THE SAD HEART
BEHIND
THE SMILE

DR. MEAGHAN MCGINNITY LONGYEAR

DISCLAIMER

This book is provided by the author and publisher on an "as is" basis, and they make no representations or warranties of any kind regarding its content. All warranties, express or implied—including, but not limited to, implied warranties of fitness for a particular purpose—are disclaimed.

The content within this book is intended for informational and inspirational purposes only. It is not intended to diagnose, treat, cure, or prevent any medical or psychological condition. This book is not a substitute for professional advice, diagnosis, or treatment from a licensed healthcare provider. Always consult with your physician, mental health provider, or other qualified professional regarding any concerns or questions you may have.

The author and publisher disclaim any liability for errors, omissions, or inconsistencies in the content and make no guarantees regarding the outcomes you may experience from applying any of the information or strategies presented. Results may vary from person to person, and your use of this book constitutes your acceptance of this disclaimer.

If you are experiencing suicidal thoughts, self-harm urges, or any mental health crisis, please seek immediate support. In the United States, you can contact the Suicide & Crisis Lifeline 24/7 by calling or texting 988. You are not alone—help is available, and there are people who care and want to support you.

DEDICATION

This book is for you. It's a message of hope, a reminder to keep going. Writing it helped me face my own triggers and limitations. Publishing it is my way of telling you—don't give up. Keep searching for answers, for balance, for peace.

If you feel lost…

If you're stuck in depression, addiction, intrusive thoughts, eating disorders, or something else…

This is for you.

You are not broken.

You are not alone.

Your story isn't over.

Your purpose is still unfolding.

This book is for you.

ACKNOWLEDGMENT

I believe in God as the Creator of all that is, while keeping an open mind about how it all came to be—and about the journey our souls take and the greater meaning behind it all. I also believe that we choose our parents, families, and friends before we arrive in human form.

I'm so incredibly grateful that I chose my parents to guide me through the early years of life despite the challenges we presented to one another. I'm thankful for the amazing family I was born into, who helped me find my true self by challenging me in ways only they could. Their unique personalities pushed me, stretched me, and ultimately helped me grow into who I am today!

I am thankful for every experience I've walked through in this life. Maybe I took the long road to get here, but at 45 years old, I have found a peace within myself that I never imagined was possible—even better than I could have dreamed of. I don't regret a single choice I've made, no matter how foolish it may have been.

These are just a few of the incredible souls I've been blessed to walk this journey with:

To Mike, my brilliant and compassionate husband—I love you the most! Thank you for believing in me, guiding me, and, most of all, loving me! No one has ever challenged me the way you have and pushed me to grow in ways I never imagined I could. I'm so grateful we found each other and recognized the work we came here to do. Healing hasn't been easy, but together, we've proven we can get through anything. Thank you for holding me up when I wanted to quit. You are my everything.

To Mom and Dad—though I always said growing up, *"I never asked to be born,"* I sure am glad I was! And I'm so thankful for your beautiful love story that brought me into this world. I could apologize again and again for all the hard times and for being a pain in the ass to raise, but we can't change the past. I believe we challenged each other so we could all grow. Thank you for loving me, believing in me, and never giving up on me—even in my darkest moments. Your words and your love kept me pushing forward. Thank you for giving me life and being the example that let me fly. I hope I've made you proud. I love you so big!

To Brandon, my kindhearted little bro—looking back, I know I wasn't always the nicest big sister, but I've *always* felt fiercely protective of you. You are such a blessing in my life and anyone who is fortunate enough to be in your presence! You have the kindest spirit and most grounding presence of anyone I know. You being in my life has made me a better person, and I'll always be thankful for that.

To Drs. Deb & Scott Walker—you created the most amazing technique in the chiropractic profession, in my opinion, and there are simply not enough words to express my gratitude. You continue to support and encourage all of us NET practitioners and share your wisdom to help us grow and expand so we can help more people. You are truly angels on Earth. Thank you for being such a pivotal part of my journey.

To Drs. Cathy & Kevin Determan—you've taught me so much and helped me explore the depth of this powerful technique and beyond! Shadowing you, learning from the way you work with patients, soaking up all the gold you constantly share—it's been a dream come true. I'm so grateful for all you've given me, for continuing to teach me, and for being two of the most incredible mentors I've ever had. I'm honored I get to call you my friends!

To Dr. Denise Parker—this entire journey began because you needed more patients for your NET Certification. Talk about the stars aligning! You helped me in a way that literally changed my life. Whatever you guided me to release that one August day was just enough to give me the hope that I *could* heal. For that, I thank you with all my heart, soul, and being.

To Jessica and Anna—I never would have survived senior year without you two. You gave me laughter and light when all I wanted was to disappear. Even though our lives went in different directions, and we are not as close as we once were, you will always have a huge place in my heart. I think of you often and send you love every time. I truly don't know if I would still be here today without your friendship. Thank you for helping me grow and for simply being there and caring about me.

And to everyone else—there are so many more people I want to thank. I could write a book thanking all the people who have touched my life! Every person I've had the pleasure of knowing has impacted my path in some way. The patients I serve, classmates, colleagues and teachers, past coworkers, and bosses—you have ALL shaped my life. Even the ones who did not like me. I'm thankful for every single one of you.

And to those that I hurt, I hope you know I was struggling with my own burdens. I hope you can find it in your heart to forgive me for the times I was unkind. Love and light to you all.

ABOUT THE AUTHOR

Dr. Meaghan McGinnity Longyear is a Chiropractor, Energy Medicine practitioner, and Medical Intuitive devoted to helping others uncover the deeper connection between the body, mind, and spirit. Through her work with Neuro Emotional Technique (NET), Chiropractic, and Acupuncture, she supports individuals in releasing unresolved emotional stress and rediscovering their inner truth.

With a background rooted in both clinical understanding and spiritual insight, Meaghan brings a compassionate and grounded presence to her work. She believes healing is not just about fixing what's broken but about remembering who we truly are beneath the pain, conditioning, and survival patterns. Her approach blends science with soul, honoring both the emotional complexity of being human and the deeper purpose behind our life experiences.

Her own healing journey—including struggles with emotional overwhelm, intrusive thoughts, and self-worth—has been the foundation for her work. She writes and serves from a place of lived experience, offering hope to others who feel stuck, lost, or unsure if healing is even possible.

When she's not working with patients, getting fairy hair, or reading metaphysical anatomy books, you can find Meaghan sitting on the beach with her husband, Mike, and her 15-year-old soul dog, Bailey!

TABLE OF CONTENTS

∞

Chapter 8

Chapter 9

Chapter 10

Chapter 11

FOREWORD

As developers of the Neuro Emotional Technique (NET), we feel the subject of emotional stress and how it affects everything in our lives is of the utmost importance. This book is brilliantly written by Dr. Meaghan Longyear, who shares her personal experience of struggling with depression and how she felt so alone as she searched for years to find the help that changed her life.

We have known Dr. Meaghan for many years, and we consider her to be a special blessing in our lives. She is a highly talented practitioner and an expert in the field of emotional stress, and there is no better person to guide you through the process of finding your path to improved health.

The world is full of challenges, and sometimes, we can end up holding unresolved stressful experiences inside us. When this happens, many different conditions can result. Some of the most common emotionally related symptoms are:

- depression

- anxiety

- feeling overwhelmed

- mood changes

- trouble concentrating

- unable to enjoy life

and the list goes on!

Unresolved stress can manifest as physical symptoms, too, and this can include chronic aches and pains, headaches, exhaustion, trouble sleeping, and stomach problems- and the truth is, stress can be a factor in almost any kind of condition. Identifying if you have an unresolved stress factor associated with your condition is key. The bigger question is probably, what can you do about it?

This informative book is a treasure that is filled with lots of valuable information and stories of how others have been helped. One of the chapters in this book explains NET and how it can help you. NET is a mind-body technique that can help release unresolved stress that is 'stuck' in your body and causing all kinds of aggravations and recurring problems. Addressing these stuck emotional stress patterns can help us heal and deal with the stress of life in a healthier way.

Dr. Meaghan is one of the most inspiring people we know, and with this book, you will gain a new level of awareness, understanding, and hope. Above all, there is hope! Dr. Meaghan is truly a gift to the healing arts, and her enthusiasm and compassion are clearly present in every word she writes.

Drs. Scott & Deb Walker

Neuro Emotional Technique

Encinitas, CA

CHAPTER

THE BEGINNING OF THE JOURNEY

*"The two most important days of your life are the day you are born,
and the day you find out why."*

—Mark Twain

L ife is full of joys, sorrows, fears, and triumphs. As humans, we each have unique experiences. We confront our deepest fears and discover our strengths, often moving through despair to find strength and resilience. Our lives are defined not only by the challenges we face but also by the courage we muster in the face of seemingly overwhelming odds.

Every heart has a story of struggle and strength, a narrative that resonates with the universal experience of being human—afraid, yet undeniably strong. This book is a testament to that human spirit, a record of my experiences through the shadows of mental anguish and into the light of understanding and acceptance.

As a Chiropractor today, I use my past experiences to empathize with and aid those around me, channeling the insights gained from my trials into helping others heal. No matter how dark my past has been, the future has unfolded into something profoundly rewarding. During this darkness, I attempted to end my own life, a stark moment in my memory, marking both an endpoint and a beginning.

Sitting in my little red Ranger at the Catalpa and Woodward Avenue intersection, I gazed at the rounded brick building that was a familiar landmark on my daily drives. Its unique architecture always caught my eye—a gentle reminder of stability in the bustling metro Detroit area, where the skies were often as gray as my thoughts. But that day, those thoughts were darker than any overcast sky.

A sudden, forceful urge surfaced as I sat there, idling at the red light, staring hypnotically at the building. It whispered relentlessly, darkly, *'End it. Do it now.'*

The words echoed, growing louder in my mind: *'Now. Now. Now. NOW. NOW. NOW.'*

It was as if my dim inner turmoil had turned into a screaming tempest, pushing me towards a precipice I had flirted with but never fully confronted.

I gripped the steering wheel, my knuckles turning white, the engine humming softly. The urge was overpowering, almost physical in its intensity, pulling me toward the very building I had admired countless times. Without fully understanding why, I found myself accelerating, the building growing rapidly in my windshield as I got closer and closer.

Then, clarity—or something like it—snapped inside me like a rubber band stretched too far. Panic surged, and with a frantic, almost out-of-body urgency, I cut the wheel hard to the left. Tires screeched in protest as I slammed on the brakes, the truck halting just shy of the ornate wrought iron fence opposite the building. My heart pounded violently against my ribcage, a drumbeat loud enough to drown out the storm in my head.

Sitting there, the truck stopped, but with my mind racing, I looked around.

'What the fuck just happened? Did anyone see that? Recognize my truck?'

Questions fired in my mind, each sharp with fear and disbelief. In the rearview mirror, I caught a glimpse of my eyes, wide with fear and realization. I had to leave the scene of my near destruction before anyone could piece together what had nearly happened.

That was the last day I ever took antidepressants. They were prescribed only a few months prior, dubbed my "happy pills," as taking them made me feel authentically cheerful and sunnier inside. They cast a warm glow over the grayer days for a while, but a darkness had crept in quietly and insidiously. It felt alien, as if it were puppeteering my thoughts and actions from a cold, distant place.

I had survived a suicide attempt before, though the memories were blurry. Dark thoughts were always in my head, but this was the second time I acted on them. This attempt was unconscious, like my body and thoughts were acting against me. Suicidal thoughts were a side effect of my antidepressant medication. Indeed, most antidepressants are known for side effects such as out-of-control actions, psychomotor agitation, and confusion, just to name a few.

My childhood was a mixed bag with both happy and sad memories. However, there was an overwhelming darkness within me, a relentless shadow. Voices that haunted and tormented me, telling me I was a disappointment. Even as a child, I obsessively sought to understand what was happening around me.

I knew which floorboards in the hallway and staircase would creak so I could sneak down the hall and listen to the adults talk after I had been put to bed. I cannot recall the things I heard or what prompted me to do it, but I remember the urgency, the compulsion to be aware of the conversations that seemed to hold some importance in my young mind. It was as if I needed to piece together the world around me to understand things I wasn't meant to hear.

Even though I wasn't always the nicest big sister, I was very protective of my little brother. Whenever I snuck down the hall, I would make sure he was safely tucked away in his room, with the door closed, to shield him from hearing anything he shouldn't. Even then, I felt a strange responsibility to carry the burden of whatever I overheard alone. It felt like my duty to keep him safe from those moments of grown-up talk, whatever they were.

Growing up, I felt burdened by a weight that dragged me into dark places. As long as I can remember, I have harbored thoughts of ending it all or wishing I had never been born. But that moment racing toward the brick building was the first time I acted on those thoughts so drastically. Feelings of failure were always close by, fueled by a constant sense of inadequacy. Though not unkind, my family had their hands full, especially after my brother's open-heart surgery. After that, everything in our house shifted. The focus turned to him—his needs, his recovery. I knew he deserved all that care and concern, but it felt as if there was no room left for me.

But there I was, a 4-year-old, unable to grasp fully why suddenly I seemed to fade into the background. I felt a need to understand and know what was happening, and it fed into that obsession with sneaking around to hear more. I do not recall much from that time except a buzzing of emotion that I can only imagine reflected my parents and family feeling all kinds of stress and worry. I didn't realize until later that I'm an empath. I feel other people's emotions very strongly and deeply. Sometimes, I mistake my emotions for those around me.

My parents, usually very attentive and loving, were consumed by hospital visits, medical consultations, and an overwhelming fear I could sense but didn't quite understand. I wasn't the center of attention anymore, and I think that's when the shadows started to grow. The weight of feeling unseen and unheard began to settle in.

On the day of his surgery, anxiety hung thick and heavy in our house. I remember packing my small red suitcase, storming out of the house, and heading to the corner of our block to "run away." I hid in the large bushes until someone came looking for me. My mom came to find me after returning from the hospital, deeply distressed that I felt the need to escape. Making my mom cry felt like just another example of disappointing someone. Doing something wrong. Story of my life. Even at that young age, guilt already clung to me, a shadow that would follow my every move.

While my father never made me feel unwanted, and my mother always had a kind word for me, it was never enough to drown out the voices telling me I was a disappointment from birth. My father, hyped up by his brothers, was convinced his first child was a boy. Though he never showed any sign of regret, loving me as any father would, the voices in my head convinced me that I was a disappointment to him.

My dad was a man who could never sit still. Even now, he's always on the move, diving into projects, running errands, or squeezing in a workout. Growing up, that energy filled the house like a constant hum, and I felt it deeply. If I sat on the couch after school, unwinding with some TV, I'd panic the moment I saw his red F-150 pull in front of our home. I wasn't afraid to be scolded; it was something subtler, more unsettling. I'd jump up as if I'd just been caught doing something wrong, scrambling for a broom or a rag just to seem busy, as if I had to prove I wasn't wasting time.

He never raised his voice at my brother or me about chores; we did what we were supposed to. But his teasing— "I've been working all day, and you guys are just lying around?"—stung more than I ever let on. He probably didn't realize how hard I took those offhand comments. They made me feel like I was never doing enough, like I had to keep up with his unrelenting pace, or else I was lazy and useless. Resting felt like an admission of failure, like I wasn't worthy of the space I took up if I wasn't constantly doing something.

That feeling lingers even now. When my husband comes home and finds me lying on the couch, there's still that nervous flutter in my chest, like I've been caught in a moment of weakness. The pressure to always be in motion and achieve something still hangs over me. It's not just about being productive—it's about being enough. And somehow, I never quite feel like I am. I am equally as triggered when I see others sitting around, not doing something. It's like I resent that they are able to rest and take a moment, but I am not allowed to. I consciously recognize that we all need to be able to relax, but my body gets tense and agitated when triggered by people not keeping busy.

So, feeling like a failure wasn't new; it had been there as long as I could remember. On the day I nearly drove into that building, all of that weight came crashing down on me. Years of trying to be "enough" finally caught up.

The guilt and self-doubt, which had simmered quietly within me for years, finally erupted all at once. There was no hiding from it anymore, no pretending that everything was fine. That constant need to prove myself, to be doing something, became suffocating. And for the first time, I couldn't outrun it.

Keeping these feelings to myself was second nature. I was private and secretive to a fault. Sharing my thoughts and feelings wasn't something I always felt safe doing; instead, I internalized everything, each thought and emotion buried deep until it festered into tears. My emotional pain would often manifest physically, and I'd put pressure on different parts of my body to manage it.

I'd grip my hair in fistfuls to make the anxious, vibrating sensations in my body just *stop*! I didn't let anyone know what was wrong; I felt ashamed of so much that I thought it better not to speak of the turmoil inside. It seemed safer to keep it all locked away. In my little world, everyone was normal; I was different. Broken.

I was raised Catholic and experienced moments of profound shame due to the behavior of priests and nuns at my Catholic grade school and church.

The Confession booth was the worst: the priest's shadowy figure behind the screen, the heavy silence that seemed to stretch on forever after I spoke, and the feeling of my sins being weighed and measured. It was as if every mistake I confessed to was another mark against me and further proof of my unworthiness. I always seemed to have Confession with the not-so-happy priests. Though I loved many of them dearly, especially Father Prus, when confessing my sins, I often got priests who scolded me instead of reminding me of God's love and forgiveness.

Like most siblings, my brother and I fought. Admittedly, I was jealous of how he stole my parent's attention. But I was made to feel cruel; I usually had to say quite a few more Hail Marys and Our Fathers than the rest of my classmates.

Then there were the times in church, sitting in the front pews, when my friends and I would get scolded for whispering and giggling. Everyone's looks of disapproval made me feel small and insignificant, reinforcing my belief that I could never do anything right. I can still see one particular Father's beady black eyes staring at me from the altar, condemning my chattiness.

Church just made me withdraw more. Talking to the priests in Confession was out of the question; I didn't want to burden anyone with my issues, especially those who seemed to embody perfection. So, I didn't. Instead, I sat in the dark box, reflecting on my regrets and fears, unable to speak for fear of the response from the holy man on the other side of the screen.

The idea of confessing my deepest struggles to them was terrifying, as if it would only confirm my worst fears about myself. How could I, with all my flaws and failures, speak to those who seemed so flawless? It was easier to keep everything bottled up and maintain the facade that everything was fine, even though, inside, I was anything but fine.

My parents were truly incredible people. They loved us deeply and provided a joyful home filled with laughter and phenomenal music! They were truly amazing, but I saw that they were hard on themselves. My dad was a marvel for his work ethic and creativity. In the construction world in Detroit, he was highly sought after and known for his efficiency, leadership, and attention to detail. His woodworking projects at home were nothing short of artistic masterpieces.

And his garden? It was so stunning that passersby would stop to admire it, some even leaving their contact information, hoping he'd call them if he ever decided to sell our home.

Despite how much people admired him, my dad never seemed to accept any praise. He would downplay his incredible talents, dismissing everyone's compliments. This baffled me as a child and later shaped how I viewed my achievements—always with scrutiny, never quite good enough. From the stories I've heard from my family, my grandparents were the same way. The apple doesn't fall far from the tree, as they say.

My mom was similar in her modesty but different in her expression. As a nurse to cancer patients, she exuded compassion and care. Her bright smile and presence comforted those enduring the most challenging times of their lives. Yet, despite her extraordinary ability to nurture and uplift, she, too, seemed to struggle with feelings of inadequacy. I often marveled at her at work—her kindness wrapped like a blanket around her patients—yet she doubted her worth and rarely stood up for herself when people were unkind to her.

This behavior—self-criticism and reluctance to acknowledge one's worth—was not lost on me. I absorbed it the same way I absorbed their love and music: entirely and without question. It was the behavior modeled at home, and I replicated it in my own life, not knowing any other way to be—nurture vs. nature.

This environment, while full of love, set the stage for my ongoing struggles with self-esteem and anxiety. Feeling unnoticed further compounded these issues. For instance, the love and attention my brother received during his surgery was necessary and understandable. But to my young mind, it meant I was less important and less deserving of attention. This feeling of being second best and insignificant would only continue.

I became someone who didn't speak up, who shrank back, who expected to be overlooked. The anxiety of not being enough, of being a disappointment, was a constant drone in the background of my daily life. As I grew older, this fear only became more paralyzing.

The silent, unspoken messages I internalized from my parents' struggles affected me despite their best intentions.

They weren't aware of the depth of my internal battles, just as I never fully grasped the weight of their own self-worth issues. We were a family bound by not only love but a shared, unspoken pain of never quite feeling good enough, each of us in our isolated bubble of doubt and self-criticism.

I never felt like I belonged or fit in with my family. Big family holiday gatherings were particularly tough for me. The air seemed thick with judgment. My insecurity about the clothes I wore and how I acted was suffocating to me. Sometimes, I found myself frozen, unable to move or interact, terrified of receiving a disapproving look for reasons I couldn't understand or being ignored and not included.

This was just how I saw the world. I always felt on edge, anticipating the next bad moment, and my imagination became a cinema of worst-case scenarios. It was exhausting.

Michigan football on Saturdays felt like a sacred tradition, almost like a holiday. The entire day was planned around the kickoff, and the atmosphere in the house was charged with emotion. Wins were celebrated with joy, but losses were devastating. The house would fall silent, with everyone retreating to their corners, quietly grieving as if something so much greater than a football game had been lost. Only later in life did I realize how deeply I had internalized those emotions.

For me, it wasn't just about the game; a loss became a reflection of my worth. If the team lost, it felt like the world was ending. Rationally, I knew it was just a game and that life would go on, but somehow, I made it my responsibility. I'd convince myself that I hadn't done the right rituals—maybe I didn't wear the lucky shirt from last week's win, or I hadn't done the hand gestures the same way.

What started as innocent superstitions morphed into this heavy burden. When we lost, I cried. Not just for the team, but because, deep down, there was a feeling inside me that I had let everyone down.

This overwhelming fear of failure didn't stop at football. It bled into everything. If I failed a test, broke something, or made even the smallest mistake, it felt like a catastrophe. Each misstep felt like the end of the world, like I had somehow ruined everything. Rationally, I knew these things were small, just part of life, but emotionally, it felt like the walls were closing in and often felt intensely suffocating.

I constantly felt as though one wrong move could unravel everything. Naturally, I began to overthink every little thing. I despised having to make a decision, convinced that I would choose the wrong thing and have to suffer the results of my choices. There was no way of coming back from it.

I was caught between worlds; I was loved, but I didn't feel I deserved it. This dichotomy became a breeding ground for chronic sadness and a relentless desire to disappear.

As a young child, feeling unimportant, especially during pivotal moments like my brother's surgery, planted seeds of doubt and insecurity that grew within me. These feelings were not merely passing clouds but persistent storms, dampening my spirits and darkening many days.

Throughout the years, my mind was often a tumultuous place. From feeling like an outsider within my own family to fearing failure in everything I did, each experience added to a warped self-image and persistent anxiety. The gulf between my public facade and private despair widened into a vast chasm.

However, this book isn't just about the battles with shadows. It's also about the glimmers of hope and resilience that occasionally break through the darkness. When I nearly ended it all on the corner of Catalpa and Woodward, my life changed. This turning point marked the end of my reliance on antidepressants and the beginning of a new chapter, where I began to navigate my struggles with more awareness and without any pharmaceutical intervention.

This book is also more than a recount of past pains; it's a message of perseverance. My life was easy and pampered compared to those in much worse situations, yet, from my point of view and emotional reality, things felt insurmountable. Yet, here I am, sharing my story, not as a tale of unending sorrow but as a testament to the human spirit's capacity to adapt and overcome. If you find yourself in a dark place, know you are not alone in your struggles! While our experiences are unique, the journey toward healing is a shared path many of us walk, often in silence.

I hope to reach you through these pages, to touch your heart and offer a beacon of light. No matter how daunting the journey seems, there is always a possibility for redemption and growth. This book is my extended hand, held out to guide you out of the shadows. Remember: the light outside, though faint it may seem, is worth moving toward.

CHAPTER

SHADOWS AND SHAMROCKS

"Family is like branches on a tree; we all grow in different directions, yet our roots remain as one."

--Suzy Kassem

My immediate family has always been my anchor. With every high and low, every moment of joy and heartbreak, I find myself drawn back to my roots, feeling the strength of the McGinnity legacy behind me. Growing up, being a McGinnity was something I carried with pride. The McGinnity Boys were legends at my grade school; everyone had a story about them, and their reputation seemed to echo through every hallway. Their athletic ability is a big one, especially in basketball! After playing all through their school days, many of them coached! They grew up in the community and were very active and well-known by our Catholic School Community. At family gatherings, I'd wait eagerly for those moments after a holiday meal when the stories would start. We'd all gather around, laughing as they reminisced about their antics and adventures.

I felt the greatest connection when listening to my family tell stories or share jokes. My great-grandmother's voice, thick with her Irish brogue, still lingers in my memory, a reminder of heritage and tradition. These family moments shaped my understanding of who I was, even as I wondered how my story would someday fit into theirs.

But as I grew, life became more complicated, and I wasn't always prepared. Watching my uncle battle cancer truly shook me. I was twelve. He fought hard even after brain surgery and countless treatments, but, in the end, cancer claimed him, marking a turning point for me and my family. He passed away at just 38. Witnessing his journey sparked a fascination with the brain for me. I dreamt of becoming a brain surgeon, as I listened quietly to the adults discussing his condition. I didn't understand everything then, but I could feel the emotions of each conversation. Losing someone taught me that family was both a source of immense strength and profound vulnerability.

The day I wore my uncle's shamrock tie to school in his honor seemed like a simple gesture. I had wanted to feel close to him, to carry a piece of his spirit with me. However, as I'll soon explain, the unintended hurt it caused reminded me that even the best intentions can have unintended consequences.

Grieving taught me how fragile family bonds can be and how easily misunderstandings can create lasting divides. I carried this understanding with me as I grew up, navigating relationships and handling my struggles. Through the highs and lows, I continued searching for connection and understanding, not only with my family but also within myself.

Watching my uncle go through surgeries and return to what seemed "normal" led me to think he could handle anything. That these McGinnity boys were so powerful! It felt like he could shoulder the burden of his illness and get back to his life. But cancer had other plans.

I remember the moment I heard the news. It was almost like an out-of-body experience. I was up later than my normal bedtime, listening to my Mariah Carey cassette tape and playing in my bedroom. Suddenly, everything went silent. I could hear my mom's footsteps as she walked to tell my grandma and dad, "He's gone." I didn't understand death, and I remember freezing, too afraid to move or make a sound. All I remember is the silence and stillness.

Over the next few weeks and months, a lot changed. I don't think anyone was quite themselves for a long time. We couldn't talk about him since it would only upset everyone. Nothing made sense to me. My uncle wasn't much older than my dad, and at that time, I thought only older people died.

Fast forward to St. Patrick's Day that same year. You must understand that my maiden name is McGinnity, so St. Patrick's Day is a big deal for us!

My dad and his brothers had taken my late uncle's clothes, and I wanted to wear the shamrock tie he always wore in March. I wanted to be reminded of him. But at my Catholic school, we wore uniforms, and, on that St. Patrick's Day, I wore my uncle's tie, wanting to uphold his memory and our traditions. I went to school with one of his daughters, my cousin, and I'd assumed she might wear something of her father's for the holiday as well. I was so excited to wear that tie, proud to be a McGinnity, and eager to show off my Irish heritage! But then I got called down to the principal's office.

I was incredibly nervous as I walked down to talk to Sister Patricia Marie. She was very kind to me and probably saw how terrified I was. She explained that, by wearing the tie, I had upset my cousin, who was still grieving her dad and hadn't known I had it. She had wanted to wear the tie herself. I felt awful. This explained why a few of my friends had been distant, even cold, toward me that morning. I hadn't worn it to hurt anyone—if I had known it would cause pain, I never would have. I would have given it to her for her to wear!

When my aunt picked us up that day, she was visibly upset, making me feel even worse. I sat in sheer panic the whole drive home, not knowing how to make things right. That moment caused a lot of tension in our big family, and we never really moved past it.

Families often ignore problems and pretend they never happened. I'm not saying this is good or bad, but it is how I understood adults to handle problems. From that moment on, I felt responsible for causing a division in our family.

As a 12-year-old, I did something I thought would bring up good memories and smiles, but it left people crying, angry, and not speaking to each other. I still feel a pit in my stomach when I remember sitting in the principal's office, the silent drive home, and the dread of my parents hearing from my aunt what I had done. This experience still haunts me, making me feel like I can't trust my instincts. Like, even if something feels right, it'll still wind up hurting people. I've had to do a lot of Neuro Emotional Techniques (NET) to write this book, as I constantly fear that sharing my story might make someone in the family upset.

The fear that I could upset someone, though I was excited to share my story to help others who found themselves in similar feelings, almost made me quit writing. Neuro Emotional Technique sessions allowed me to recognize the fear, sometimes knowing exactly what I was upset about and other times just feeling the tension in my body and fuzzy feelings in my head, and allowed me to work through the pattern of belief I was clearly stuck in. I worked on how badly this affected me from such a young age to still feeling like that paralyzed child, afraid to move forward for fear of hurting someone in my family that I loved.

By the time I was 18, I was partying hard and often recklessly with my friends. On "Bike Night" in downtown Royal Oak, we'd hop on random guys' bikes and ride around with them even though they were strangers. I'm grateful something up above was watching over me and that I was never abducted or assaulted. I craved attention, and this was how I was getting it. My insecurities were mounting, and my self-esteem was low. I drank, trying to keep up with the people around me. I wanted to be the life of the party. Indeed, this was what I grew up with!

I had watched my family and neighbors having a good time in the backyard, drinking beer, laughing, and dancing to music. I thought I was replicating what I'd seen in my environment—don't most people do that?

But my brother took a different path; he didn't follow the drinking craze like his big sister. He'd drink a bit, but nothing like what we grew up seeing. He was more like my mom. I wanted to be more like my dad: having fun, telling jokes, and being the center of attention at parties!

I knew Mom worried about Dad. Like many families, we drank to celebrate the good times and drown out the bad. When I sensed Mom was worried or upset, I did what the oldest child often does: I tried to make things okay and improve everything. I remember picking flowers for her, cleaning the house, or making her little presents.

I needed her to be happy. Whether it made me feel safer when she was okay, or I didn't want her to worry, I'm not sure. But I remember the anxious, buzzing feeling I'd get inside when she wasn't okay and how overwhelmed I felt trying to fix it.

After work, on some Fridays, my dad would go out with his construction crew in downtown Detroit. Without cell phones back then, my mom would be anxious and worried about him getting home safely. A friend who knew where they were—just letting off steam, playing pool and darts—would sometimes take me down there so I could make sure Dad got home safe.

Then, I'd head out with my friends to drink at a buddy's house whose parents were at the bar every Friday night, giving us a place to party! Many of my friends' parents went to the bar on weekends, so this felt normal. I knew my parents would be asleep when I got home from partying so that they wouldn't get mad at me. This Friday night cycle went on for a long while.

Dad and I had some great conversations on those rides home, but I always worried if the week had been particularly challenging for him and his crew, especially since they had been drinking. I couldn't help but worry how he would be on that drive. I personally don't handle liquor well and tend to become very aggressive, feeling like I'm towering over everyone and ready to fight anyone who dares to challenge me. It seems like most of my family members struggle with it as well. Perhaps it's a common trait among the Irish, in general.

I admired my parents and wanted to be like them in different ways—the good and the bad. I smoked cigarettes like my mom and drank beer like my dad, and I felt so proud when people said I was just like them!

Even now, when my husband says, "You're your dad's daughter," I feel the same pride. I didn't know any different about the drinking. I saw the fun that drinking brought to them, their friends, and our family, and I thought it was natural. Isn't that the case in most families? Most of my friends' parents were the same way, so it was a widely accepted behavior that I excused with, "I'm Irish!" whenever I got sloppy drunk and acted like a fool.

On the other hand, my brother didn't seem to appreciate how stupid we all acted—remember, he's the "bright one" in the family! He didn't go for drinking and partying, and I would sometimes judge him for that. I feel a lot of regret for the way I treated my brother growing up.

When I finally decided to quit drinking, I gained some clarity. And when I started getting Neuro Emotional Technique done, I gained some freedom. Living in shame over our past actions can cause dis-ease in the body—it's not healthy to hold those issues in our tissues.

3
CHAPTER

SCHOOL DAYS STRUGGLES

"Ships don't sink because of the water around them; ships sink because of the water that gets in them."

—Unknown

School was always a struggle for me. I often felt insecure, like I was on the outside looking in, unable to find my place in the classroom or on the playground. I never felt safe and comfortable in my skin.

Though I adored my kindergarten teacher and fondly remember her kindness, she often pulled me aside for talking too much. I wasn't trying to be disruptive; I just had so many thoughts and things I wanted to share! However, instead of encouraging my curiosity and enthusiasm, some teachers labeled me as a distraction, making me feel like I was doing something wrong simply by being myself.

Academically, I was just slightly above average, mostly coming in as a C student. No matter how hard I tried, I couldn't seem to achieve the higher grades I wanted. Over the years, I developed test anxiety. During tests, I'd always doubt myself and second-guess what I knew to be true.

My report cards were filled with comments like "motor mouth" and "talks too much." I felt like I was continually falling short of others' expectations, with my parents often reminding me to hush up in school. But I was a social butterfly and had a lot to say! Though my parents always laughed about my ability to go on and on about any topic, my teachers didn't always have the same forgiving attitude. Socially, I had many friends but struggled when they would ditch me to hang out with someone else or when we would get into quarrels.

Typical grade schoolgirl stuff, right?

Well, at the time, it was crushing! I couldn't let go of little things like not being asked over to someone's house, yet I hated sleepovers and would often want to go home! This conflict between wanting to be included and being scared to leave my home was enraging. I would get so angry at myself! Why couldn't I be like everyone else? Why was I so afraid all the time?

My beautiful cousins always seemed confident and put together, excelling in everything they did. Whether it was academics, sports, or social situations, they appeared to navigate life effortlessly. I couldn't help but compare myself to them. They were everything I wasn't: smart, confident, athletic, and pretty. I felt like I was constantly living in their shadow, trying to measure up but always falling short.

I loved getting their hand-me-down clothes but always felt I wasn't cool enough to wear them. I even tried playing basketball and softball, but my athletic abilities were severely lacking! However, I started cheerleading for the grade schoolboys' basketball teams and felt a rush of excitement! Although I loved cheering as an outlet for my passion and energy, it also brought out some body issues since I wasn't as developed as the other girls.

In first grade, a cute boy smacked my butt as I was walking down his row. I completely froze, terrified to walk by anyone after that. I always felt nervous coming in front of the class and became hyper-aware of my body and how others perceived me. I still have moments of self-consciousness, although they are not nearly as paralyzing as back in grade school. But even to this day, I still prefer sitting in the back of the room to melt into the sea of faces and not stand out.

Instead of focusing on my strengths and abilities in school, I was preoccupied with not measuring up to my cousins or classmates. This mindset affected my self-esteem, making me feel even more isolated and misunderstood. I understand that I wasn't the only girl in school who felt this way, but this intense obsession consumed my thoughts and often enraged me when I couldn't perform as well academically and athletically as others.

Despite these challenges, there were moments of light. I was chatty and loved to put on plays, act, and sing! In fifth grade, I was in the finals of our school's Declamations Contest. You had to memorize a poem and act it out. I chose 'Sick' by Shel Silverstein and I could probably recite it and act it out still to this day!

I was terrified sitting on the stage in front of a gymnasium filled with 5th- 8th graders—not to mention all the parents and teachers! Even in this big moment, my mind wandered; I was a daydreamer, often lost in my thoughts and fantasies. I remember the girl next to me saying loudly, "They are calling your name! It's your turn!"

I quickly returned to reality and somehow walked out to the microphone, trembling with fear. I saw my dad in the back of the gym and instantly felt my fear turn into excitement. As the provider for the family, he worked a lot, so it was a big deal that he was missing work to see me. He was smiling big, visibly proud of me. This helped release a lot of my fear at that moment!

I looked at him during my performance and didn't forget a single line! When I finished and sat back down in my little seat, I felt good—trembling but knowing I had nailed it, just as I had practiced so many times in front of my mom and my Aunt Gerri.

Once again, I was lost in my thoughts as they announced the winners: 3rd, 2nd, and 1st place. The girl next to me snapped me back to reality so I could accept the 1st-place trophy. What a moment!

Now that I had won this contest, however, I expected myself to win each year. But I didn't. I didn't even make it to the finals. I was so upset I couldn't even appreciate how great it was to have won in 5th grade. This is how a lot of accomplishments for me have gone. If I succeed, I soon enough can only focus on keeping that success going. If I couldn't repeat it again and again, it felt like failing. This was how the negative thoughts and negative voices began to grow—kind of like in the old cartoons where people would have an angel and devil perched on each shoulder. The devil was emerging as the louder voice in my head.

As school went on, these dark voices only grew more powerful. As I said, despite my efforts, I was consistently a B-C student in most of my classes, never quite reaching my academic goals. My teachers often told me I could do better, yet my grades stubbornly remained the same. Each report card reminded me of my inadequacies, confirming that I wasn't giving it my all.

My brother remembered everything he read and did well in school. He even tutored me when I was in high school, and he was still in junior high! I always admired how smart he was. School seemed to go so easily for him, yet we both had our struggles. It is interesting how we dwell on our own shortcomings as though others don't have them, too.

Whenever I received a report card with C's or heard a teacher's comment that I could do better, the dark voices grew not only louder but more insistent. However, my parents would often remind me that they, too, were C-average students in school. Not everyone is an academic genius, they'd say, and I had other gifts. But I couldn't see those gifts; I could only see what I was not enough of.

I still hated myself for not getting better grades. I excelled in church choir and acting in school plays. I wanted to be an actress or singer when I grew up! But sitting in the classroom day in and day out, struggling to stay focused and learn material, was dull and felt useless to me.

I would lie awake at night, replaying moments of the day in my mind and berating myself for not being smarter or more diligent. I wondered why I couldn't understand the material as quickly as my classmates or how my efforts didn't translate into better grades. The disconnect between my hard work and academic performance was a source of constant frustration and self-doubt.

In class, it felt as though I floundered while everyone else effortlessly floated along. No matter how many hours I spent on studying and doing homework, the results were the same. I began to internalize this, believing that my value was tied to my academic success or lack thereof. The dream of being a heart or brain surgeon someday drifted away when I realized how much more school I would have to endure.

And let's not even talk about getting called on in class to have to answer a question or read out loud. Sheer panic. Terror pulsing through my veins, cold but burning like ice. I remember when we would have to read assigned passages of material aloud in class. I would count to my paragraph and mentally recite my section over and over in my head in a cold sweat, desperate not to stumble on my words.

But the only class I felt drawn to was English! I enjoyed writing papers and expressing myself. I was also pretty good at math and had a passion for algebra. But I never seemed to be able to focus on the things I excelled at, only where I was falling short. And so, the internal narrative kept growing: I just wasn't good enough.

The voices in my head whispered that I was a disappointment, that I was not working hard enough, and that I was bringing shame to my family. These thoughts were pervasive and affected every aspect of my life. Group projects, classroom discussions, and even casual conversations about grades filled me with dread.

I vividly remember the feelings of panic at parent-teacher conferences. My teachers would say I talked too much in class and needed to focus more. They would point out that I often seemed distracted, didn't participate enough, and that my scores were not as good as they could be. They weren't wrong; I was a total daydreamer! I fantasized all the time, often getting caught up in visions of joyful things I would rather be doing than sitting in class, feeling stupid.

I thought I was a burden, that my parents deserved a better child, someone who was more like my brother, and that I was failing almost fundamentally as a person. I believed these thoughts over anything else others offered. It is not like my parents told me that I wasn't enough or that I was not doing well. They were my parents; they were encouraging and very supportive, but their voices were not what my brain listened to.

In hindsight, I realize that my academic struggles did not define my worth or determine my future potential. However, it was nearly impossible to see beyond the immediate pressures and fears at the time.

I attended a Catholic elementary school and then a public high school. Only about five of my grade school classmates attended that high school, and in a freshman class of over 400, I felt overwhelmed and uncomfortable.

Going from wearing uniforms to dressing in the latest trends and fashions was traumatizing. Though I was pretty skinny, I would wear baggy jeans and T-shirts because I felt uncomfortable in my skin. I have never had a fashion sense, so I would get picked on for the outfits I put together— striped pants with a floral shirt, for example. I liked how I dressed, but I felt like a fish out of water trying to dress the part at this new school.

By the time I reached my junior year, my depression had intensified, leaving me desperate to fit in and feel less alone. My grades were a constant source of frustration and disappointment. I would do anything to feel like I belonged. Friends came first, and with that came experimentation and making choices based on this need for acceptance. However, I was paralyzed in fear of judgment in group settings. Even though I started smoking cigarettes my freshman year, I refused to smoke or eat anything in front of people. I felt so different and awkward.

In my senior year, a misunderstanding within my friend group led to a very lonely and uncomfortable time. The group I had been a part of for years turned against me, leaving me isolated, as even those who still wanted to be my friend avoided me for fear of causing more drama. This social turmoil was exacerbated by several incidents that spilled over into my home life: kids from school vandalized my parents' property and made prank calls to my house, causing tension between my parents and me.

Then came a pivotal run-in with the police. I had fallen in with a new group of friends who weren't the best influences. We confronted the girl who wouldn't listen to my side of the story one night. We marched in, and one thing led to another, and then the police were called. I had been drinking, and so I failed a breathalyzer test. Teenagers aren't allowed to have any alcohol in their system, so they took me to the police station to call my parents.

In my drunken state, I was beyond terrified of disappointing my dad. I pleaded with the police not to call my parents, begging them to drop me off on a corner so I could walk home. But they were firm, explaining that they had to follow the law. I didn't know what to do or say to get them to listen to me. I knew they had to follow protocols, but I wanted this thing to end without any consequences. I even tried opening the car door so I could jump out to either run away or die.

In my desperation, I told them that if they called my parents, I would kill myself, leading them to place me on suicide watch. I found myself sitting in a small cell with glass windows, horrified of eventually facing my parents. The anxiety was overwhelming. I kept praying to God for a way to disappear, for the floor to open up and swallow me, for the roof to fall on me, for something, *anything* that would get me out of this situation. When I realized there was no escape, I bashed the back of my head against the concrete wall, hoping to end my life and avoid confronting my parents. The tension between us had been building for months due to the ongoing school drama, and I knew they were at their wits' end.

The moment I saw my dad at the police station is one I'll never forget. I had to use the bathroom, and as the police officer escorted me down the hall, there was my dad. The disappointment on his face was devastating, and his words, "Remember us?" with his twisted look of disgust, are something I don't think I will ever be able to forget. I've always felt like a failure to my parents, teachers, and pretty much everyone in my life. This was the final nail in the coffin of my self-hatred. I had always struggled with suicidal thoughts, and this incident brought them out in a visceral way.

I felt defeated, worthless, and a burden to everyone around me.

Living felt like too much to handle. The constant feeling that I couldn't do anything right and that everything I did seemed to affect someone else was too overwhelming. While typing this, I realized I still have a lot to process from that night. My stomach physically hurts remembering the moment I saw my dad's face.

The voices in my head told me I was a failure, I was ruining my family's reputation, and I would never amount to anything. They reminded me of every mistake, every disappointment, every time I had let someone down. I was crushed, suffocating under all these insecurities.

The night wasn't over, though. Rather than going straight home from the police station, I had to stay at a hospital overnight so doctors could run tests and talk to me about my suicide threats. I dreaded the moment I would be discharged from the hospital. I do not recall being picked up the next morning and driven home, but I can still feel the sickening feeling in my gut as we drove home in silence.

'What are my parents going to do? Say? If I'm not grounded for life, maybe they will ship me away.'

Life had been pretty bad for me lately. I didn't want it to get worse. Social situations were minefields. I was terrified to walk down the halls alone, always needing someone to accompany me. Even the mere thought of entering a store alone would paralyze me with fear. So, I would only go into places if my mom or a friend were by my side. This anxiety extended to my job as a nurse's assistant at Beaumont Hospital during high school. Despite being a hard worker and having a strong work ethic instilled by my parents, I never felt like my efforts were enough. Compliments from colleagues and supervisors felt hollow; I always believed I could do and be better.

I was bullied at school and dreaded walking down the halls alone. Whether cruel comments, being screamed at, or being pushed by people I once had called friends, these incidents left lasting scars. Each encounter further reinforced my poor self-esteem, telling me that I was worthless and didn't belong anywhere.

When I finally embarked on my healing journey in my mid to late 30s, one of the most significant milestones was realizing that I could sit in restaurants and walk into stores without fear. This might seem like a small feat to most, but for me, it was monumental! When we first met, I used to envy my husband's confidence in attending a movie or lunch alone. I still vividly remember the day I walked into a restaurant alone for the first time without feeling that familiar paralysis. At all. It was incredible!

It was a simple act, but it symbolized so much more. It represented freedom from fears that held me back for so long. The process of healing was slow, a gradual peeling away of layers of depression, anxiety, and self-doubt. This newfound confidence wasn't an overnight transformation; it resulted from persistent effort and self-reflection.

As I continued to heal, I also noticed changes in other areas of my life. I started feeling more at peace with myself and more comfortable in my skin. Tasks that once seemed impossible became manageable, and I began to take pride in my accomplishments, no matter how small they might seem to others. The ability to walk into a store or sit in a restaurant by myself is something I still get excited about today. It's a reminder of how far I've come and the progress I've made in overcoming my fears.

Looking back, I realize that my early struggles were crucial to my journey. They shaped me into who I am today, instilling a resilience that has carried me through countless challenges. The voices in my head may have been harsh and critical, but they also pushed me to seek my strengths and work tirelessly to improve myself.

This process of healing and self-discovery is still ongoing. I still experience doubt and fear, but I've learned to face them head-on, armed with the knowledge that I am capable and worthy. My journey through school was brutal and beat me down into a dark hole of suicidal thoughts, eating disorders, and cutting. It wasn't until Chiropractic School that I realized these struggles I had previously wrestled with had set me up for invaluable lessons about perseverance, self-acceptance, and the power of resilience.

As I continue to navigate my life, I carry these lessons with me, using them as a foundation to build a future where I can thrive. The path hasn't been easy, but looking back now, I know every step has been worth it. Each small victory is a testament to my growth and the strength I've found within myself. And for that, I am deeply grateful.

CHAPTER

THE YEAR OF HELL

"Behind every sweet smile, there is a bitter sadness that no one can ever see and feel."

—Tupac Shakur

That night seemed like the longest night of my life. The arrest, the disappointment of my parents, and ending up in the hospital as a suicide risk. It was all so intense. I felt like I was trapped in some nightmare that would never end; part of me even dreaded its end because I was so scared to face my parents.

'What are they going to say? Will they hear me out?' I kept wondering. The next thing I knew, it was dawn, and I had to go home to face the music.

My parents and I talked at the dining room table. The police and doctors suggested that my parents look for a journal or diary of mine in hopes of understanding what I was going through since I threatened to take my life. They wanted to see if there was a record of any previous thoughts concerning such actions. It was quite the confrontation, like a moment of judgment exposing all I had been concealing for so long. The discussion was heated and emotional as they tried to connect the picture of their child with the reality in front of them. From my journal, they'd learned what I had done and the depths of my depression.

I didn't know what to do with myself; I was lost in despair, shock, and self-hatred. My parents were shocked, angry, and worried about me. So, they decided the proper response was to ground me, supposedly to give me time for reflection, but it only felt like punishment for my choices and actions.

Instead of partying with friends, I spent a lot of time at home under my parents' vigilant eyes. The freedom I had grown to take for granted was a memory. My parents would closely monitor my activities to ensure that I did not fall back into the same behavioral patterns that led me to my place of desperation.

I had to confront the reality of my life choices and their repercussions for my family. The trust had been shattered, and I felt utterly incapable of repairing the damage I had caused. I had to acknowledge that my actions had consequences, not only for myself but also for those around me. The lies I had spoken and the secrets I had kept had created a chasm between me and my parents, and it would take a significant amount of time to bridge it. All this, of course, culminated in my first suicide attempt.

During the diary reveal, nobody screamed or yelled; I remember the conversation being very direct. We were all pretty much in deep shock about the whole scenario. I still remember my parents being appalled at the things I had been doing secretly—drinking, having boyfriends, cutting myself, sneaking out, and partying in places that were pretty terrible for good Christian children like me.

I didn't think I could feel any worse than the night before, but listening to all my most private thoughts and insecurities read aloud had sent me into the darkest hole I had ever been in.

I remember sitting in my empty room, my parents having taken everything I loved as punishment and leaving me with just a mattress and my clothes. I wanted to run—running had always been my answer to everything. I was, all at once, a child again, unwanted and desperate to be loved.

To escape. I longed to escape.

"Run!"

The one-word answer that always made sense.

Every day was just another struggle to get up and face the world. I felt even worse after my suicide attempt, like a burden to my family. The isolation and punishment of being grounded only deepened my sense of worthlessness. There was tension in every minute at home. My parents watched me like hawks, trying to prevent another crisis. Of course, their vigilance was understandable, but for a seventeen-year-old, it was suffocating. I felt like a prisoner in my home, caught and trapped by my actions and their consequences. The gap widened between myself and my parents, and I could not see how it would ever close.

The emotional toll was simply overwhelming, culminating in physical pain. I'd sometimes struggle to breathe. The pressure on my chest was intense and crippling.

The nights were the worst. I was alone in my room, replaying these scenes repeatedly in my mind. What I had done, whom I had hurt, and the secrets I had kept seemed to whirl around in an endless circle. Sleep was elusive and, when it came, filled with nightmares that left me more exhausted than before.

I was numb, sure that I wouldn't come out on the other side of this unscathed. The house phone was being monitored, but the harassing prank phone calls still came into our house every evening and often while we were all asleep. The bullying never ended. I was alone with no way out, and I couldn't bring my parents any more pain than I already had.

Had my parents kept a gun in the house, I'd have used it to kill myself. I knew that my dad had some knives for fishing and utility purposes, but I was too scared of the pain as well as the possibility that I just wouldn't complete the job. I was afraid that I would be found bleeding and that things would just replay themselves.

So, I turned to the only remaining option: the medicine cabinet. I didn't know what pills I was grabbing, but I knew my dad had some prescribed pain medication from an old injury. I gathered whatever I could together into a little Ziploc bag and planned to overdose on it. I snuck back to my room and started writing notes to my parents, brother, and close friends. I told them I was sorry for being such a disappointment and causing so much pain and frustration in their lives. Over and over, I wrote, "I'm sorry" and "I wish I had never been born."

It was as if I were standing beside myself, watching me write those notes. I didn't shed a tear while writing them, but now, reflecting on it, I am sobbing. But back then, my despair and hopelessness were so deep that I was beyond tears. I'd thought about this for so long but never actually felt horrible enough to really do it. I swallowed the pills, one handful after another, until the bag was empty. I don't remember exactly how many, but in my journal, I recorded the number as being around 70.

After writing the notes and taking the pills, I sneaked past my dad, who was sitting in the living room watching TV, and went downstairs to sit with my mom in the basement. Although she was mortified by my decisions, she still showed compassion and allowed me to sit with her. We sat there, talked, and listened to music, just like we used to before my adolescence. It was a pleasant moment—what was going to be my last memory—and I thought about how I would never again feel that familiar shame and humiliation. No more disappointing my parents or emotional torment from within. I truly felt free for the first time in my life.

After some time, I went to bed and lay down peacefully, believing it was all finally over. I left my mom with a hug and a kiss after beginning to feel dizzy and lightheaded.

And then the next thing I know, it's 5 a.m., and my alarm clock is ringing. In my bedroom, my stomach hurt, and my head was pounding.

'What the fuck?!' I thought. *'How am I alive right now?'*

It couldn't get any worse; I was such a failure that I had even failed at killing myself.

'You've got to be fucking kidding me!'

Despite all the pain, I got up and got ready for work. Who the hell could I tell I tried to kill myself? It would just bring more problems. So I trudged off to my job as a nurse's aide at the hospital, trying to keep up appearances. I felt like vomiting during the shift nurse's meeting. I found myself racing down the hall but couldn't make it to the bathroom before I started throwing up. The physical pain was unbearable, and the emotional toll was worse. How does this happen to me? You would figure this was my rock bottom, and in many respects, it was.

Things gradually changed after that. I made friends who stood up for me, and my senior year became bearable. I was making it, but barely. At 18, I started skipping school with my friend, Anna. That spring, we wrote ourselves out of class often and spent the warm El Niño days swinging at the park and drinking coffee colatas. Those senior year memories are some of my most cherished.

Anna and I sang together in the choir and acted in Drama Club, which was one of the highlights of my senior year. I had performances and choir trips with amazing friends who didn't judge me by my past and didn't believe the lies about me. After feeling alienated for so long, this was a major lifeline. We created so many memories, reminding me that life can still have periods of joy and laughter.

All through that, though, my emotions stayed so raw and intense. Despair, self-hatred, guilt—all there, munching on me. But little slivers of hope would peek through—moments when I could glimpse some future beyond the darkness. The road was not over by a long shot, but each step forward helped restore a little of the lost trust. Every day was a struggle with anxiety, and the future felt so overwhelming. These feelings, as painful as they were, had become part of me. They were me, defined me, and eventually made me very guarded.

As my classmates chose colleges and professions, I lacked a clear vision of what I wanted. And my GPA wasn't much anyway. I was also terrified of leaving for college, feeling like the girl at the sleepover who's afraid to be away from home.

But the memory of this time reminds me of how far I have come. It was an adventurous ride from pain and despair to growth and interest. I had trust to rebuild, wounds to heal, and small steps to take. Each of the small improvements represented a major victory, even if I didn't always see it. This experience, though harrowing, has taught me the valor of perseverance and that the human spirit is strong.

I always had an early curfew, and most nights during the week, I could not leave the house when all my friends did. My friends would be out making happy memories while I was stuck at home, depressed. My parents thought they were protecting me, but it felt overwhelmingly punishing to be separated from all of my friends.

It isolated me because I couldn't do what my friends did daily. It meant I was a loser, missing critical times and conversations. The fear of missing out became a clear, distinct cause of my stress. Knowing all of my friends were together, and I was sitting at home carved my gut with anxiety.

Angry and depressed, I would hang out in a small hideaway in our garage attic, a small space where I kept my magazines, journals, and other things that would bring me some joy. No matter how hard I tried, though, I couldn't stop feeling cut off from my friends. I obsessed about it non-stop.

The worst part was hearing everyone's stories and inside jokes the next day at school. I would hide in the garage attic or the basement alone and angry, doing stuff like drinking my dad's beer and cutting during my sophomore and junior years of high school.

Once, I had a huge crush on this boy who asked me to Homecoming. I was so stoked, but that thrill turned into devastation when he went with someone else because I was never allowed to hang out with him outside of school.

'Why are my parents so strict? They are ruining my life! I haven't done anything to deserve this!'

These thoughts consumed me and further eroded my confidence.

I didn't think I had given my parents any reason to doubt or distrust me. But in trying to protect me, they only were hurting me by keeping me home and preventing me from making my own choices. Locked up, I rebelled and learned to lie and sneak. I felt like I was two separate people: one for my friends and one my parents saw as their daughter.

I must have told my parents I'd seen *Waiting to Exhale* in the theatres at least five times. Yet, to this day, I have never actually seen the movie. Instead, I was partying with my crush or girl friends.

The boys I dated in high school always felt out of reach, like I was chasing after something I couldn't quite grasp. Deep down, I never felt good enough for any of them. My self-esteem was so fragile, so desperately tied to the idea of being loved and accepted, that I can see now how I pushed them away. I was always searching for validation, always afraid I wasn't enough. I clung too tightly, always anxious they'd leave, convinced that any moment they'd find someone better.

And if I was drinking, I'd eventually find myself in tears, sobbing about how unworthy I was, convinced they were cheating on me or on the verge of leaving me. It became a painful cycle where my need for reassurance drove me to question everything. Looking back, I cringe, but I also feel for that girl who just wanted so badly to feel accepted. And honestly, I'm so relieved we didn't have cell phones and social media back then. I can only imagine how much worse it could have been if my life were displayed online.

In the spring of my senior year, my friends and I drove to confront another girl who had been spreading rumors about me. Of course, we had alcohol in the car. When we got pulled over, fear washed over me as the police lights flashed behind us. I was already on probation from being caught earlier that year, so all I could think of was how it would disappoint my parents all over again.

We were lucky that night; my best friend Jessica, who was driving, hadn't started drinking, so the officers took our beer and let us go with a warning. Since I was 18, they didn't call my parents; instead, they just gave me the Minor in Possession of Alcohol ticket, leaving me relieved but deeply rattled. It was yet another brush with the law. Another situation where I felt as though I was dragging everyone else down. I was thankful to have my friends by my side, but I couldn't shake the feeling that it was all my fault.

I couldn't bear to go through the court process alone, so I told my mom about it, even though I knew it would upset her. It was like this dark cloud just followed me wherever I went, and, increasingly, alcohol was always part of the picture. This time, the judge ordered me to do community service and attend AA meetings. I dreaded it. I had family members who had been through AA, and while it worked for them, they also jumped to other obsessive behaviors to fill the void.

I felt uncomfortable listening to strangers share their stories and open up about their struggles in meetings. Even Al-Anon, which I was also recommended to attend to give me exposure to family members worried about other family or friends who have a problem with alcohol, left me feeling raw and exposed. Many people find healing and community in AA, but for me, it was like standing in front of a mirror and being forced to confront issues I wasn't ready for. Eventually, I started having random people at parties sign my AA attendance forms to meet the court requirements. I knew it was wrong, but I couldn't bring myself to sit in those meetings anymore. It was too much, too real. At that time, I was not prepared or equipped to handle the reality of my reflection in the lives of others.

The experience with AA informed my decision to avoid using the program when I eventually quit drinking years later. Still, I'm grateful for its support for so many others on their path to sobriety! Over 17 years later, I remain alcohol-free, and I've found other ways to support myself through the ups and downs of life.

I struggled with my body image constantly through high school, wishing I looked like someone else—anyone other than me. Hyper-focused on my imperfections—small boobs, a big forehead, and a lack of curves. I always felt like I needed to be skinnier, even though at 5'3", I never weighed more than 102 pounds. I compared my weight to my friends, starved myself, and restricted my eating to very small, planned amounts throughout the day. A box of Gerber baby cookies and a Dunkin' Donuts coffee became my "normal" diet. Family dinners were my only full meals, not because I wanted to eat but to avoid raising suspicion from my parents. When I would binge on food, I'd desperately try to make myself vomit to prevent gaining weight, though I never could. Later, in chiropractic school, I learned why that was physically difficult for me, but back then, it was just another reason to feel broken.

Looking back now, I see how all these moments, big and small, were part of a larger journey. My teenage years were full of pain, confusion, and a desperate longing to feel understood. I can see now that my parents were doing the best they could, even if their efforts sometimes fell short in my eyes. My dad, especially, had a tough time navigating the emotions of raising a teenage girl after growing up in a house full of boys. The gap between what they were capable of and what I needed felt unbridgeable back then. Control, isolation, and emotional turmoil only pushed me further towards suicide.

Those experiences taught me lessons that have remained with me ever since. Feeling excluded, struggling for independence, and fighting with self-worth are chapters in my growth story. They helped me reflect on how much strength it took to survive my emotional reality and how much perseverance was needed to survive my life as a result.

CHAPTER

THE TURNING POINT

"Mental Health problems don't define who you are. They are something you experience. You walk in the rain and feel the rain, but you are not the rain."

—Matt Haig

I have been immersed in the medical world for as long as I can remember. My mother was an oncology nurse, and I can remember childhood summers spent in her office, surrounded by the sterile smell of antiseptic and the quiet hum of machines. While most kids were out playing in the sun, I was inside, sketching pictures with bright, colorful highlighters. These weren't just any drawings; they were small tokens of hope and joy for the patients enduring the harsh realities of chemotherapy. Even at that tender age of around eight years old, I found something deeply fulfilling about bringing a smile to someone sad or sick. As an empath, I could feel their anguish, though I did not understand exactly what they were dealing with.

The desire to help others wasn't just a fleeting childhood fantasy; it was deeply rooted within me, and as I grew older, it only became stronger. During high school, I found myself working as a nurse's aide. I wanted to follow in my mother's footsteps so much, to wear the same scrubs and lab coat and to carry the same quiet strength she did. But there was one problem: needles terrified me. The very sight of them made my stomach churn and my palms sweat. It was a crippling fear, and it forced me to reconsider my path.

My struggle with depression, a shadow looming over me my whole life, led me to another idea. I could help others who felt the same darkness I did. I decided to become a psychologist. It seemed like the perfect fit—a way to heal the mind rather than the body. But as I sat in those psychology classes, learning theories and practices, I felt a gnawing doubt. The thought of spending my days listening to others' sorrows while I struggled with my own was overwhelming. I didn't want to be the one sitting across from a patient, trying to solve their unhappiness when I couldn't even figure out my own. It felt too close, too raw, too much.

So, I shifted directions again, this time to law enforcement, where I could make a real difference. The idea of protecting people, of being a force for good in the world, was intoxicating. I imagined myself as a beacon of hope, helping those in need and bringing justice where there was none. But reality has a way of creeping in, often in the form of wisdom from those who have walked the path before you.

My college professor, a retired cop, saw through my naivety. He took me aside with a kindness I didn't fully appreciate until later and shattered my idealistic vision of the job. He painted a picture not of heroism but of the work's gritty, often heartbreaking truth. It wasn't about saving the day but about surviving it. It takes someone very strong and special to handle the rigors of a job like that and keep their sanity. For his warning, I am thankful to my professor who saved me from a future that would have left me more broken than whole. This gave me even more respect for the men and women in Law enforcement and any criminal justice career.

At this point, I was weary. Weary of school, of changing directions, of feeling lost in a sea of choices that all seemed to lead nowhere. I had spent so much time chasing after anything that would give my life purpose, and getting nowhere in my search was making me doubt myself. I felt adrift, anchored to nothing.

A guidance counselor once told my mother she should be a nurse. This gave her direction, and she pursued it. It was the perfect career for her! My father dropped out of architecture school when it did not feel like the right fit for him, and shortly after, a family friend employed him as a journeyman in construction, eventually reaching an apprenticeship. My parents' clear, direct guidance led them towards success. I wanted the same! I *expected* the same!

When I started at my local community college, I accumulated knowledge even though I had no idea what I wanted for my future. I had no passion for anything, just desperation. After four years of college, I took a year off. I'd studied two subjects and felt drawn to neither. I was depressed, and my boyfriend was telling me to figure it out because he didn't want to marry someone who didn't have a college degree.

I'm sure you can imagine what that did to my self-worth. Though he was only speaking his truth, I felt like not only was I floundering, trying to find "my purpose," but now a potentially exciting future with this amazing guy was in jeopardy! I scrambled in desperation, asking everyone in my life for guidance.

"What should I do? Tell me what I should be!"

But no inspiration came, so I got a bachelor's in business administration. I graduated, but there was no joy, just relief that it was over. Though I did not marry him, in retrospect, I am thankful for that conversation because it pushed me to finish my degree, saving me time ten years later when I pursued my doctorate in chiropractic!

Meanwhile, I drifted from one receptionist job to another—mostly in medical practices. Though I had a passion for helping others, I couldn't find a way to turn it into a fulfilling career. Employers called me a "Jack of All Trades," but it only made me feel more lost.

I knew a little about a lot and helped keep the offices flowing, often by being placed wherever someone was needed. Filing, answering phones, and scheduling appointments didn't fulfill me, but I needed a job. During this time, I lost myself in drinking and partying. It seemed normal; everyone around me was doing it, so I didn't think much about it. It was just part of life, or so I told myself.

One night at a pool bar down the street from the hospital where I worked, I met him—my future husband. He was the new manager behind the bar, but since I got close to the former bartender, I didn't like him! None of us regular patrons did. He was cute enough, but replacing someone, losing my bartender, and, not seeing him at the end of my work days was actually pretty tough. Just one fewer place where I felt accepted.

However, the new bartender and I struck up a friendship that lasted for years before it turned into something more. From his "wingman" to his wife, what a journey it's been! Looking back now, I realize that he was the shift I desperately needed in my life; he began to help me piece myself back together without even knowing it.

We were both broken in our own ways, each carrying our burdens and scars. Early on, our relationship was very reckless—we laughed, stayed up late, and masked our pain with Miller Lite, trying to drown out the darkness within. It felt like we were running from our demons, finding comfort in each other's chaos. But behind the laughter and late nights, there was always an undercurrent we couldn't ignore—a gnawing realization that distraction could only last so long.

Eventually, I realized that running from our problems wasn't the way. Therapy wasn't new to me. Since my arrest,

I'd bounced from one therapist to another, almost like clockwork, searching for something—anything—that could offer relief. I sat in therapy rooms that all looked the same—sterile walls, rattling furnaces, tissues within reach. The intention was always to heal, but more often than not, it felt like stepping onto a battlefield where my thoughts turned into enemies. I'd return home exhausted, only to fall back into old patterns, clinging to the chaos we shared because it was easier than facing the truth.

Every session followed the same course: the therapist would ask how I was feeling, prodding me to share what was on my mind. Though never at a loss for words, I struggled to find the right ones to make sense of the turmoil within. But as the minutes started ticking away, the words would start spilling out faster until I lay everything bare—my fears, insecurities, that darkness that seemed to follow everywhere. I would share the sorrow that clung to me like a shadow, the crying nights into my pillow, and the reckless decisions to dull the ache.

Although I hoped to find solace, I left most of those sessions feeling more lost than before. It was as if talking about my feelings only fueled the flames, raising the fire higher, reminding me with every word how deep the darkness ran and just how hopeless everything felt. They would listen, with their furrowed faces or slight nods, before giving their advice. Coping strategies, breathing, ways to reframe my thoughts—nothing ever really reached the core of what I was feeling.

I would leave the therapist's office feeling raw, as if I had reopened a wound I was trying so hard to heal. All this emotional exposure, all this airing of my deepest fears and sadness, drained me to the point where there wasn't anything else to think about except my wanting to end it all. I had come to dread those sessions. And the irony wasn't lost on me: therapy, a supposed tool for healing, was turning into just another reminder of how broken I felt. I never felt understood in my sadness, more so judged by all that I revealed, which hid me away from wanting to share all that I felt.

There were days when, once the session was over, I would sit in my car, gripping the steering wheel tightly to hold back tears. I used to stare outside the windshield, watching people go about their lives, feeling like an outsider looking in, my body buzzing inside. The therapy wasn't helping, but it was making me more acutely aware of the void inside me. I continued to go back week after week, hoping that maybe something would click this time. Perhaps this time, the therapist would say something that made everything make sense.

That frustration began to seep into every part of my life. I had done everything that was expected of me—I came for therapy, talked about my feelings, and tried to work out the problems—but instead of getting any better, my depression worsened. Talking, analyzing, constantly reflecting—everything seemed to push me further into the darkness.

At those desperate moments, I would further distract myself with reckless behavior. The nights out, the drinking, the parties. They became my escape from it all, something to try and quiet the storm in my head. I'd drink until I couldn't think anymore, until the world became a blur, and the pain was numbed, even if only for a few hours. But it would always be transitory, with sadness catching up with me in the mornings.

I am deeply grateful that social media wasn't as omnipresent then as it is today. I can't even imagine what that would have looked like if those moments of raw vulnerability—those nights where I was the crying drunk girl at the party spilling her sadness to anyone who would listen—had been captured on someone's phone and shared with the world. For me, immortalizing those moments on the internet is terrifying to consider.

Somewhere inside me—deeper in than I will probably ever be able to reach—I realized that I couldn't keep living this way. I knew the answer wasn't drinking every day until passing out, but for now, it was all that kept my mind quiet. I was out of control, and I knew it.

Many mornings before I started dating my future husband, I woke up in strange places, hardly recalling how I had arrived there. Stumbling home early in the morning or driving myself home drunk at night, I was relieved to have somehow gotten home but terrified by how close I could have come to disaster. Even thinking about what could have happened now makes my blood run cold. I'm so very lucky I never got raped, abducted, or worse, on those careless nights.

I knew I had a drinking problem long before I was ready to consciously admit it to myself. At first, it didn't feel like an issue. When I was out with friends, drinking was just part of the routine—another way to bond, to blow off steam, to fit in. But, after a while, the social excitement failed, and I withdrew. I didn't want to be around anyone anymore, not even at the bar. Instead, I'd stop at the liquor store on my way home and grab a 12-pack to head back to the solitude of my home.

At first, I told myself it was easier this way—no need to dress up or converse. But the truth was I was isolating myself, and the drinking had taken on a different tone. I wasn't drinking to have fun anymore; I was drinking to numb myself, to drown out the feelings and thoughts I didn't want to face. Ten beers a night became my new normal. The next day, I'd be back at the liquor store, buying another 12-pack after work, embarrassed but unable to stop.

I'll never forget one evening at the liquor store just down the street from our house in Sterling Heights. The owner, who had gotten used to seeing me, smiled and casually commented, "Heading to another party tonight? You've got some stamina, drinking like that every day!" He didn't mean anything by it—just small talk—but the words hit me like a punch to the gut. I wasn't going to a party. I was going home to sit alone in my silence, with nothing but a case of beer and a couple of packs of cigarettes to keep me company.

After that, I started rotating between different liquor stores so no one would notice how much I was buying. I pretended everything was fine, but deep down, I knew. I needed alcohol all the time. Even trips to Home Depot weren't complete without a beer in hand. I justified it with the same excuses every alcoholic makes. I'm young. This is how people relax. I'm having fun.

I was drinking because I didn't know how else to escape the constant sense of not being enough, of never measuring up. Of being a piece of shit with no future ahead of her. Eventually, that feeling became too big to push away; no amount of alcohol could drown it out anymore.

I knew I stood at a precipice, and things needed to change. I didn't know how. I had tried quitting drinking before. Many friends who didn't drink anymore would offer to hang out and do things with me, just not at the bar. I just knew the therapy wasn't working, booze was making me feel like shit, and I was racing down a bad path. I didn't want to live like this anymore. As many times as I had failed to quit or cut back before, I felt so lost on how to achieve what I thought I knew deep down was necessary. Not being afraid of dying left me hopeless that I would ever be able to get out of this hole I had dug myself.

One evening, I went to my favorite bar, Snookers Pool & Pub on Woodward Avenue, as I usually did after my Tuesday therapy session. There was always that enlivening feeling of being with my people who were in the darkness with me. That night, something was different. The therapy session I had just come from was particularly shocking. Unlike the others I had seen for all those years, this therapist, who I had seen for a couple of months now, said something that struck a very deep chord. I wish I could remember exactly how she phrased it, but it was something along the lines of, "By continuing to drink the way you do, you are condoning your family's history with alcohol."

It was like she had taken a 2x4 and smacked me upside the head. I just sat in my truck outside her office, her words echoing in my mind, their impact hitting me harder with every passing second. I awoke to the shadow of my family's history looming over me. It hit me like a ton of bricks: unless I changed, I'd keep making the same mistakes.

I realized at that moment, sitting in my truck, that I needed to stop drinking.

My body was nearly paralyzed from fear of quitting. I was afraid of actually giving up alcohol, to face life without the crutch that I had all these years. Then there was the daunting task of telling the man I'd been dating for about a year—the man I was in love with—that I needed to make this huge change.

The thought of losing him because of all this made my stomach twist in knots. I thought he was going to think I was utterly insane. I thought quitting the partying lifestyle would end us. What kind of fun would we be if we weren't going out, drinking, and living it up? I clutched the steering wheel tightly, mustering the courage to talk to him once I got inside.

I finally pushed open the bar door, and the smell of beer and cigarette smoke hit me, along with the low murmur of voices. There he was, cleaning glasses behind the counter and finishing his shift. My Miller Lite bottle with a maraschino cherry on the top was sitting at the front of the bar. He prepared it for me every night. He looked at me and gave me that warm, loving smile that made my heart race. I could barely return the smile tonight. I walked up and sat on one of the stools at the bar, my hands shaking as I set them on the counter.

"Hi baby," he said, coming forward to kiss me. His eyes scanned mine. "You look like you've seen a ghost. How was therapy?"

I swallowed hard and tried to find my voice.

"It was different this time," I finally said, nearly in a whisper.

He furrowed his brow with concern, moving closer toward me. "What happened?"

I hesitated, feeling the thudding of my heart in my chest.

"Well, she said something that got to me. She said... she said I'm condoning the history my family has had with alcohol by drinking like I do."

His eyes locked onto mine, and I watched his concern deepen. Neither of us spoke for a moment; the weight hung between us. I was nearing tears quickly, but I quashed them down, not wanting to break in front of him as I had done so many times before.

"So, what does that mean?" he asked, his voice gentle.

"It means," I said, my voice trembling. "That I think I need to quit drinking. I cannot keep doing this if I want to break this cycle I'm in. But I am so scared. I don't know if I can do it, and I am afraid you will think I'm too much, that I am too broken to be with."

He didn't say anything for what seemed like a long time, and my heart was pulsing at the thought of him walking out. Slowly, he let out his breath, his eyes never leaving mine.

"So you're just gonna quit? Cold turkey?"

I nodded, my throat tight. "I think I have to. But I know it's going to be really, really hard. And I get it if you don't want to be with me because of this."

He rocked back a little, nodding, his face unreadable. "So you're just going to stop drinking altogether?"

My voice was shaky, but I replied, "I don't know. I only know I cannot go on like this. I'm scared, yet I don't want to lose you, either, although I don't want to lose myself. I've been losing myself for a long time now."

"You aren't going to lose me," he said and hugged me tightly.

I felt the hot tears start sliding down my cheeks.

"I know, I know, it's a lot. But I can't keep numbing myself with alcohol. It is killing me! I need to stop, and I am scared that I will spiral even lower if I don't. And I can't ask you to change your life for me, but…"

He cut me off, his voice getting more urgent now.

"But I want to change. For myself, too. I have been thinking about this for a little while now—about how much I drink now since my cousin died last year."

"You've been thinking about this too?"

"Yeah," he said, scrubbing the back of his neck. "I didn't want to mention anything because I didn't want to sound like a buzzkill. But if you're ready to stop, then maybe it's time I stopped, too. For my reasons, not just for you."

The relief was immense, but inside me, there was this thread of fear—fear of failure, fear of what that meant for us. "But what if we can't do it? What if it is too hard?"

He moved closer to me, grabbing my face, his eyes holding mine with fierce determination.

"Then we fight through it together. I am not saying it will be easy, but I'm in it with you. We will make a pact—one year. No drinking. And see what happens."

I searched his face for a trace of doubt and saw only resolution.

"You think we can do this?" I asked very low.

He nodded, then leaned in and kissed me.

"Yeah, I do. But we've got to stick together, okay? We've got to be each other's support. When one of us is tempted, the other has to be strong. Deal?"

I nodded and took a big breath, my heart pounding.

"Deal."

And that was how we decided. One year, no drinking.

We began our year on January 1, 2008, when I was 27 years old. The first few weeks were the hardest. Liquor seemed to mock us everywhere—at restaurants, parties, even at home. There were moments when one of us would reach for a drink out of habit, then stop and look at the other, a silent question hanging in the air. Our weekly Sunday afternoon lunch dates at Mongolian BBQ revealed a surprising benefit: our bills were drastically lower without alcohol! We saved so much money that first year! Our favorite waitress was happy about our newfound sobriety, but we felt guilty that our once-huge bill had now become so small.

It wasn't just the habit of drinking we had to break—it was also filling the void. I had seen others do it: some threw themselves into religion and prayer, while others worked out constantly or surrounded themselves with people. For us, that void-filler became Dove chocolate and Butterfinger candy bars.

My husband, who was bartending night shifts then, would stop almost every night on his way home to pick us up our sweets. He used to laugh about how embarrassed he was to be ringing up these candies so often, half-expecting the cashier to one day slide some Metformin across the counter. It became our little routine, a treat to look forward to at the end of the day. I'm sure we paid the Butterfinger CEO enough during those years to fund a new jet!

When we moved to Texas and consciously tried to change our lifestyle, we got better about our sugar habits, but sweets remained our go-to in times of stress. It wasn't until we quit drinking that I realized how much sugar is in beer and how deeply intertwined that craving for sweetness was with our old habits. Yet, sugar became our new comfort. Our vice had shifted.

When we moved to North Carolina for my husband's new practice, we found a new obsession: Starburst candy corn. We devoured them the way we used to drink: we'd eat until we felt sick, unable to stop. Just like with alcohol, moderation was impossible. Addictive personalities were our deeper struggle. Addiction has a power like that.

On my 28th birthday, about three months into our sobriety pact, we were out together celebrating my special day. I struggled. I am a hardcore birthday self-promoter and used to go all-out to celebrate the day as loudly and cheerfully drunk as I could! I didn't know how to do that without alcohol. My husband knew it, too. I could see it in his eyes—that longing, that struggle. I could feel the itch in the back of my mind, the desire to have one drink, to feel that familiar warmth wash over me. There was a liquor store next to the store we had just come out of. We sat in his F-150 silently for a few moments.

"I'm struggling," I said quietly.

"Me too," he said.

"I keep thinking, just one drink, it won't hurt. But I know that's a lie," I said, with the familiar feeling of just giving up like I had done time and time before.

He nodded, his jaw tight. "Yeah. It's like. It's calling to me."

He turned and took my hand in mine. "We can't do it. We made a promise. To ourselves and each other. We can't break that."

I squeezed his hand, searching his eyes for strength. "I don't want to break it, but damn, it's so hard!"

"I know," he said, his voice shaking. "But we're stronger than this. We have to be."

We left the parking lot and ventured somewhere new to make fresh memories for a birthday celebration. Not talking much didn't feel so lonely, though; the silence between us was warm. We were united in mute determination.

Six months into this journey, we realized we couldn't go back to casually drinking. It wasn't something we could control. We'd come too far, grown too much, to let alcohol back into our lives.

"We can't do it," I said, looking at him seriously. "We can't go back to drinking, not even occasionally. It's just not safe for us."

He nodded, completely understanding. "I agree. It's just not worth the risk. We found so much more in each other and in life without it. Let's keep it that way."

It was a hard decision, but it was the right one. We had found strength in each other and ourselves, that we weren't willing to give up. Quitting alcohol was the hardest thing I've ever done, but it's also been the best decision I've ever made. It saved me and strengthened our relationship in ways I never could have imagined. We turned from being just two people into a team, living full and real lives. We found enormous dreams to chase after.

And for that, I will always be grateful.

CHAPTER

DISCOVERING NEURO EMOTIONAL TECHNIQUE (NET)

"The key to healing the body is to heal the mind."

— Bruce Lipton

I was unsure of my future, going this way and that without a clue as to which direction I was heading. My husband was enthusiastic about finishing his Sports Medicine degree. But I had misgivings.

My family viewed chiropractic with skepticism after my Dad had a bad experience with one after a fall on the job site. Everything changed, however, when I saw the chiropractor treating my husband. At first, I was skeptical. But my neck was stiff, and I could not turn my head left at all. And, since my husband was practically dragging me, I went to see him. I was hesitant and still had doubts as to whether chiropractic even worked.

It wasn't what I had expected; this chiropractor was really great, unlike the one my dad had seen! I could completely turn my head with zero pain in no more than three adjustments. In the past, it usually took up to three weeks to get better on its own. This fast recovery was astonishing; it completely changed my outlook toward chiropractic care.

Only when I started to see some real tangible benefits from this treatment did my fears and doubts truly begin to dissipate. It was then that my husband and I discussed the differences between him pursuing a Physical Therapy degree or a Doctor of Chiropractic degree. Our chiropractor helped to answer questions and guide us in this big decision we were contemplating.

His wife was a physical therapist and often expressed that she wished she could write her own treatment plans instead of having to take direction from the Medical Doctor managing the patient's case. That made sense to us, so after visiting a school and learning about the philosophy of chiropractic, my husband applied to Parker University in the Great State of Texas!

Our lives changed by the time we moved to Texas. We were two years into our sobriety and newly married, embracing a completely different way of life. We did food cleanses, ate healthy, quit smoking cigarettes, and added daily running and workouts into our routines. We were much healthier physically now. I landed a job as a paralegal with a medical laboratory company, which was a huge advancement in my career. But, even with all these positive changes, I could not get rid of my depression and a feeling of futility inside me.

I couldn't understand why, after having done everything "right," the suicidal ideation that I'd fought so long and hard against reemerged. I struggled to navigate these feelings, given that everything about my life, in principle at least, should leave me feeling happy and fulfilled. I went back to a therapist, which only perpetuated the emotional chaos I had been going through. We tried hypnotherapy, which just triggered me more and left me feeling like I was spinning out of control with my thoughts.

Through that darkness, I struck up a friendship with my boss, Summer, who is now my best friend with whom I have the most elevated conversations. It all started with a book Oprah recommended, *Many Lives, Many Masters,* by Brian Weiss. The book sparked discussions that challenged my old belief systems and expanded my visions. This was a pivotal moment that I did not realize at the time, but I can now see how it helped me on the path I had always desired to find.

A couple of months before my husband's graduation, he began telling me about one of his classmates who was learning this incredible treatment method. She was studying to become certified in Neuro Emotional Technique, or NET, and needed patients to practice on. He had told me about his experience years prior when he was in his first trimester of school and had made it sound so fascinating that I immediately wanted to try it! He explained that NET is a combined approach between the mind and body that finds the physiological origins of stress-related conditions.

Unlike conventional therapies, oriented only on the conscious mind, NET finds and releases unresolved emotional stress in the mind and body. This energy, often locked into our muscles and tissues, can manifest in physical symptoms and emotional disturbances long after the initial trauma or stress has passed. The technique includes muscle response testing: a method whereby the practitioner applies light pressure to a muscle, usually in the arm, to identify areas of stress or imbalance in the body. It's based on the knowledge that our bodies store physical and emotional experiences.

If something traumatic or even remotely stressful happens to us, and we fail to fully process it, our limbic brain logs that memory, and our bodies hold on to that emotional energy. Over time, our bodies will often begin to express it as chronic pain, anxiety, depression, etc. NET works by finding those points of stress, uncovering the underpinning emotions, and then letting them go so the body can balance and heal properly, as it divinely knows how to do.

I didn't know exactly what NET was or how all this worked in the mind and body, but my husband had seen how hard it had been lately for me and thought this could help. I was excited to finally try it, even though I had tried so many therapies and treatments over the last fifteen years with very little success. But with all the things I had tried in the past, I never gave up trying other ways. What did I have to lose?

The NET session with Dr. Denise was transformational, as though she was tapping into deep, hidden reservoirs of pain and stress that I had long buried. I started crying—deep crying on the spot—an unstoppable release of emotion. Not the crying that makes you feel empty and hopeless afterward but, instead, purging something heavy and dark that has been eating at me for years.

Just about as suddenly as the tears had come, they stopped. The need to cry disappeared, and then this slight sense of tranquility and clarity was in place. That profound sadness that generally followed such emotional releases for me did not materialize. I felt lighter, as if this huge burden had been lifted.

How amazing! It was surreal that such a significant change could happen in such a short amount of time.

For the first time in many years, I felt there might be a way out of this cloud that had been following me everywhere. NET treatment opened my eyes to how intricately our bodies and emotions are woven together. It planted a seed of curiosity and possibility, which continued to grow into something much more significant later in my life.

Before the NET session, I used to be different: I would be stuck in an unshakable sadness for days after crying over something like a sad ASPCA commercial with an animal suffering. But this time was different: the emotional release was deep, yet it didn't drag me down into a pit of despair as I remembered a painful memory. In the following months, I realized that the things and people who used to set me off in an intense emotional manner were no longer doing so. I wasn't being triggered as much.

NET provided me with something that all my years of traditional talk therapy couldn't. A shift, a change in my perspective. I may not have had a background in neurology or anatomy to understand the mechanics of what was happening inside my mind and body, but I knew this was huge. Deep down, I knew this could be the key to helping me manage my depression in a way that nothing had before.

Before the NET session, life in Texas had not been as joyful as I imagined, even during what was supposed to be some of the happiest days of my life! I specifically remember the drive down I-35 in Texas en route to South Padre Island, where we would get married. It should have been one of those exciting and euphoric moments—a day that most girls dream of and plan for their whole lives.

Yet, instead, I found myself consumed by a deep sense of dread and depression. Things were exciting and thrilling: being sober, getting married to someone who truly cherished and loved me, and finally moving out of Michigan to a warmer, sunnier state, a dream I had since my teenage years. Yet my mind was still full of negative vibes, convinced that something was wrong.

We had moved in February from a particularly cold wintry Michigan to Texas, dropped our stuff in a little apartment, and then started the long drive to South Padre Island, where we would be getting married! It snowed from Dallas to Austin, which hadn't happened in over thirty years. So, here I am, crying at the thought of standing on a beach in Texas in my little wedding dress while it was freezing cold. When we pulled onto the island, it was raining and sleeting. Of course, that was my mindset: always expect the worst.

I remember trying to perk up my mood with my favorite tunes while driving to our wedding destination. I replayed Sugarland's "It Happens." Singing along exhilarated me for a minute and diverted my mind. I remember wanting to believe these words—to *live* them, not just feel them for that moment.

Fast-forward to today: I'm driving to work; that song comes on shuffle. I chuckled this time as I finally lived the life those lyrics described. I still have my frustrations and triggers—life happens, but now the lyrics strike a whole new chord. I've gone through some profound transformation, most especially with Neuro Emotional Technique, which has made me perceive my environment entirely differently.

Although it has taken many years with all the other techniques and therapies I have tried, NET helped move those blocks in my path so I can see clearly. No longer looking through the foggy lenses of past traumas, both big and small, I've been able to heal and chase the dreams I once only held as a faint glimmer of hope. Thinking of that drive to my wedding, I am surprised by how much I've grown and how much has changed since when that song would make me dream of a different reality.

After my husband's graduation in Texas, we moved to Charlotte, North Carolina, to start his new practice. Although the relief I had found through NET was great, I could not find a local practitioner who offered the technique.

The closest was an hour and a half away, and with me being the breadwinner since my husband was still setting up his practice, I couldn't afford to take time off from work to make that commute all that regularly. Without access to NET, I felt the despair sneaking up on me. My depression began spiraling once more, with the isolation of working from home only adding insult to injury.

I spent a significant portion of my day alone, and without the emotional stress relief I had experienced after just one session with NET, I began spiraling back into a state of despair.

My husband received an offer for his dream job, which required him to relocate to Atlanta to assist his mentor in reopening a neurology clinic at Life University. We seized this opportunity as a fresh start and embarked on the move. For us, it meant beginning anew, potentially accompanied by changes in our surroundings that could alleviate our financial difficulties.

In Atlanta, we discovered something that would change everything: Life University had a Neuro Emotional Technique Club on campus. Once again, the thought of having access to NET lit some spark within me, almost like at that first session with Dr. Denise. Did this opportunity to move to Atlanta allow him to have his dream job? Or for me to find my purpose?

My high school friend recently enrolled in college and was always raving about the differences between school now and when we despised high school. He seemed incredibly excited and fulfilled by this new challenge in his life. It was uplifting to witness his passion and the future goals he discussed after graduation!

Between listening to him and seeing my husband thriving with learning more and more functional neurology from his mentor, allowing them to help the patients coming to their clinic who had been previously told by their MDs, "This is as good as it gets." Yet, the changes they were making were restoring people with *hope* and allowed me an ember of fire inside that I could help other people with depression. I had to learn this technique!

At 36, I applied to Chiropractic School. It was challenging because I doubted myself and feared failure. But this time, I had a clear purpose and inner conviction that this was right, despite the voices telling me otherwise.

I wanted to learn NET, not only for my continued healing but so that I might be able to bring this incredible therapy into the lives of others. It was another turning point in my life, showing me the direction and purpose I had searched everywhere for.

CHAPTER

THE JOURNEY BACK TO SCHOOL

"I think the saddest people always try their hardest to make people happy. Because they know what it feels like to feel absolutely worthless, and they don't want anybody else to feel like that."

— Robin Williams

Enrolling in chiropractic school at 36 years old felt like standing on the edge of a cliff, peering down into the unknown, unsure if I'd fall or fly. The decision, though pivotal, didn't happen with a grand revelation. Instead, it felt like stepping through a door I hadn't even realized I'd opened. My friend from high school, now pursuing his bachelor's degree, was my biggest supporter. His excitement about learning again, about the challenge and fulfillment it brought him, was contagious.

At the same time, I witnessed my husband thriving in his career, helping patients who had been told their conditions were hopeless and watching him bring light back into their lives through his knowledge of functional neurology. All of it was inspiring, but it was also terrifying.

The fear I felt was overwhelming at times.

I questioned everything: my capabilities, intelligence, whether I was too old to start over. There was no rallying cry from my family or my in-laws. They weren't against it, but they weren't encouraging either. The doubts were louder than the support, especially the ones I had about myself. I thought about the other students who would be younger, quicker to grasp the material, and more confident in their abilities.

I feared I wouldn't measure up. The voices in my head whispered constantly, *"You're not smart enough for this. What makes you think you can do it? You are going to fail. It's what you do."*

Despite all this, something in me kept pushing forward. Perhaps it was my stubborn streak, the part of me that refused to give in to others' doubts about me. It was like I had blinders on, and I kept stepping forward somehow.

Once I was in the program, there was no turning back.

My schedule was relentless. It wasn't just the academic rigor that weighed heavily, but life outside of school, too. My husband, who was immersed in assisting in building the neurology clinic on campus, was often unavailable. While he supported me in every way he could, there was constant pressure to perform. Weekends, which once felt like a refuge, were now filled with studying, trying to keep pace with the grueling coursework.

I lived in constant tension, constantly feeling one step behind everyone. The pressure to excel and grasp the material deeply came from both internal and external comparisons. I compared my husband's brilliance to my struggles.

It appeared as if he had sailed through his education, effortlessly mastering concepts. While he was a tremendous help in breaking things down for me and my classmates, his explanations often made me feel inadequate in comparison. I would watch him explain something complex in a simple, digestible way, and it would only remind me of how far I felt from that understanding. It wasn't jealousy but rather a deep sense of frustration with myself—the same way I would feel in high school when my brother tutored me.

'Why couldn't I grasp things the way he did? Why does it take me so much longer for me?' These thoughts gnawed at me constantly, feeding into the fear I had started with. The fear of failure never left; it lurked in the background, reminding me of the stakes.

Despite the challenges, though, something kept me going—that small but persistent part of me that whispered, *"You've got this,"* even when everything else screamed the opposite. It wasn't easy to hold onto that voice when I was exhausted, staying up late, and trying to force the material into my brain.

There were moments when I would think, *'Maybe this is too much for me. Maybe I should just quit.'*

But then I would remember why I started. I would think about NET and the transformation I experienced after that day in Dr. Denise's office, how something inside me had shifted so profoundly. I was doing this to help others find that same shift and guide people through their healing as I had been guided.

The struggle wasn't just about mastering the coursework or keeping up with the program's pace. It was about learning to accept that I wouldn't do it perfectly. I would struggle and stumble, but that didn't mean I wasn't capable. I had to learn to silence the constant comparisons to my husband, other classmates, and colleagues and focus on my own journey. It wasn't about being the best or the fastest learner but about showing up daily and moving forward, even when it felt impossible. I was able to find my unique gifts through the process and then use them to help others!

I had never truly been prepared for the academic rigors of chiropractic school. Coming from a business administration background, I was walking into a completely foreign world— navigating subjects that felt miles beyond anything I had ever tackled. Radiology and Pathology, in particular, were the stuff of nightmares. Our professors were brilliant, and their expectations were high. They didn't just want us to pass; they wanted us to become exceptional doctors. Their exams were brutal, designed to ensure we understood the material inside and out—no shortcuts, no half-answers. They were grooming us to be at the top of our game because one day, our patients' lives would depend on it.

For me, it wasn't just Radiology and Pathology that presented a struggle. Anatomy & Physiology, along with Neurology and Musculoskeletal classes, were monumental challenges. With all its intricate systems, the human body felt like an enigma I constantly tried to unravel. My business background had nothing in common with learning the Latin names of muscles or understanding the complexity of how our organs functioned together.

It was as if I was being asked to learn an entirely new language, and I was far from fluent, but was extremely fascinated despite the difficulty. Something about the human body captured my curiosity deeply, and that interest, though not enough to make the material any easier, fueled my drive. I wanted to know more, even if the learning process was very slow and sometimes torturous.

I unexpectedly received profound support from my classmates. Feeling out of place due to their age and recent undergraduate education, I formed study groups and made friends. Their patience and camaraderie helped me cope. Some upper-quarter students, in particular, were lifesavers early on.

They had been where I was, overwhelmed and struggling, and they knew exactly how to help. I'll never forget the times Lydia, my first NET friend, would come to find me in the library, panicking over an upcoming exam, and offer to do a Neuro Emotional Technique on me to calm my fears. Those sessions worked wonders—not just because of the emotional release but because it reminded me that I wasn't alone in this journey. I was part of a community. She worked on me often and helped me learn the technique, and I made some HUGE breakthroughs with her compassion and guidance!

Then, my peers, especially those who quickly absorbed the material. They would sit with me and share their unique memorization techniques, breaking down complex topics in ways that clicked for me. I had been out of school for over a decade, so I had to relearn how to study effectively. My classmates helped me re-establish my study habits, and their support and patience became an anchor during those difficult times. It was humbling, yet comforting, to lean on others when I was used to navigating challenges independently. I still sing the songs Hilary and Kelli taught me to remember orthopedic tests!

But the support didn't end with my peers; the mentors I found throughout my journey were just as crucial to my success. My favorite school Advisor, Dr. Numeroff, was a constant source of positivity. Whenever I met with her, I walked away feeling lighter, more motivated, and more confident that I was on the right path. She made every obstacle seem surmountable, and her cheerfulness was infectious. This always gave me a renewed sense of excitement, even when the weight of the workload threatened to crush my enthusiasm. The positivity cards in her office always supplied the perfect message, which was needed when I was in her presence.

Dr. LaMarche, another mentor, inspired me. I attended his speech at my husband's school's philosophy event after he started his classes. Though I knew nothing about chiropractic, I was captivated by his words. He often spoke to my classes, sharing personal stories about how chiropractic transformed his life and his son's. His passion was evident—he lived and breathed chiropractic. He reminded me of my journey's purpose, the body's healing power, and the hope we can restore in those who have been given up on. His electrifying speeches reignited my excitement and reaffirmed my path.

Then, there was Dr. Determan, who taught the Basic NET course once a year at my school. His seminars were game-changers for me. As I slogged through the grind of daily classes, it was easy to lose sight of why I had enrolled. NET was my passion and reason for pursuing chiropractic, but the endless exams and grueling coursework often dulled that spark.

But every time Dr. Determan came to teach, the clouds parted, and I could see again. His passion was infectious, and his knowledge seemed boundless. He reminded me why I was there and rekindled the excitement I had felt in that first NET session before the heavy weight of academia had taken its toll. I couldn't wait to learn more from him each time he taught us!

Another key figure was Dr. Amodio, the Advisor for the NET Club on campus, who taught us how to do the technique. I remember one session vividly—a 13th-quarter student was our example case during NET Club with Dr Amodio, processing the trauma of not making the JV football team in high school. It seemed trivial initially, but as he relived the memory, I watched in awe as his body responded, beads of sweat soaking through his dress shirt. This high school memory was connected to his subconscious belief that he could not be a good doctor.

The experience was powerful, showing me how deeply these emotional traumas can affect us, even years later. It was a humbling reminder of the emotional depth NET could reach. Every session I witnessed, every student who found release reinforced my dedication to learning this incredible technique.

Of course, no one influenced me more than my husband. His brilliance and passion in neurology, understanding of the brain, and effortless explanations were sources of both inspiration and frustration. He would drop these "neuro nuggets," as we called them, little insights that opened my mind to how much trauma shapes our health. He sees a bigger picture than most and can explain it in a way anyone can understand and apply, both doctor and patient. He always jokes that "there's no such thing as emotions," but I knew that deep down, he understood their profound impact, even if he masked it with humor. He has always supported me, and once he started attending NET Seminars with me, he realized how much our emotions play a pivotal role in our brain's capacity to heal and need to be addressed, despite what might be taught.

His mentor, Dr. Hall, became another guiding light for me. Dr. Hall had this unique way of thinking, and I often left the gatherings they hosted at their clinic feeling inspired and completely overwhelmed by how much I still had to learn! He would put things together in a way that made real-life sense. Then, break these concepts down to challenge us to think deeper, allowing us to push ourselves to be better and look at things from unique perspectives. Far beyond what we were learning in the classroom. Men's brains vs Women's brains was the topic one particular evening, and though I had heard Dr. Hall talk in seminars before, this was a game-changer discussion!

He would point things out and then ask us questions to get us engaged and thinking. He talked about how different our brains are and how that affects our ability to manage stress. Men need to go throw weights around in the gym, while women need to go on a walk with a girl friend and talk it out! Something about this conversation really resonated with me, and shortly after, my friend Kelli and I started walking and talking every day for at least 30-45 minutes after classes ended.

Through it all, I realized just how much the emotional brain governs every part of who we are. It wasn't just about learning anatomy, physiology, or techniques but about understanding the human condition on a deeper level. The emotional layers, the traumas we carry, the way our minds and bodies interact—this is what excited me most and what kept me going when the academic challenges seemed insurmountable.

DD Palmer, the founder of chiropractic, talked about these three things---Traumas, Toxins, and Thoughts---interfering with your body's ability to self-regulate and self-maintain. He called these subluxations. In my opinion, a subluxation is a disconnection in achieving health and purpose. For me, the emotions or thoughts were the biggest interference, creating disconnection in my life, health, and well-being.

Now, as I navigated the intense demands of Chiropractic school, my mind became a battleground. The pressure to perform, the constant worry about failing exams, and the relentless academic demands seemed to grow heavier with each passing quarter.

Anxiety became my constant companion, gnawing at the edges of my sanity. There were moments when the darkness crept in so deep that I wondered if I could keep going. All this was bringing up the familiar suicidal escapes. I wasn't just facing stress; I was facing thoughts far more terrifying— moments when the idea of giving up seemed all too tempting. Often, I thought about getting drunk just to cope. I struggled with my sobriety a lot in Chiropractic school.

This was when I truly leaned into the power of the Neuro Emotional Technique. While it had already played a significant role in getting me to this point, it became a lifeline during those darker times. Every Wednesday, without fail, I attended the NET Club on campus. Sometimes, I even skipped class to be there, knowing that my mental health and ability to manage anxiety mattered more than anything. I would meet up with fellow students, practicing NET on each other as often as we could, sharing in each other's struggles and triumphs.

It was a powerful experience. Access to this technique allowed us to tap into the emotional undercurrents driving our stress, fear, and doubt. The more I incorporated NET into my routine, the more I felt a shift—not just in my mood but in my perspective. I even started attending out-of-state NET seminars in my second quarter, where I would immerse myself fully, getting treated and practicing on others who had been doing NET for decades. It was the only thing that balanced me as I trudged through the heavy academic load.

At every NET seminar I attended while in school, I focused on becoming "congruent" with my fears, which meant becoming emotionally aligned with my challenges. I worked on statements like "I'm okay passing exams" and "I'm okay passing Boards," but also the harder ones: "I'm okay failing exams" and "I'm okay failing Boards." The first time someone suggested the statement, "I'm okay failing Boards," I broke down into tears.

The thought of failure was so terrifying that it unraveled me in the session. Working through it, releasing those emotions, and continuing to address them through NET helped me face those fears.

There were moments during my studies that reinforced why I was pursuing this path despite the struggles. One of those moments came during a particularly challenging quarter. I failed my pathology midterm; the class was notoriously difficult. Everyone, from my classmates to my advisors, suggested I drop the class and retake it the next quarter. Dropping the class meant delaying graduation, falling behind, and watching my peers move on without me. That idea alone felt like a punch to the gut. School was my full-time job and the plan was to graduate before I turned 40. I wasn't ready to give up. Just before starting Chiropractic school, my husband and I were introduced to Dr. Joe Dispenza's work. He was teaching about the power of the mind, meditation, and how your thoughts create your reality. I was skeptical when my husband first suggested attending a weekend seminar. I was convinced I couldn't meditate, that my mind was too chaotic, too full of anxiety ever to sit still long enough for meditation to work.

But something about Dr. Dispenza's story changed my perspective. He had been in a horrific accident, shattering his thoracic spine. Doctors had told him he might never walk again. His story struck a deep chord with me because it mirrored my father's recent experience. My dad had also suffered a devastating accident; he had been bicycling when he got hit by a distracted texting driver. My dad's injuries were catastrophic—he shattered his spine, femur, and other parts of his body. Like Dr. Dispenza, he was told he shouldn't have survived.

Listening to Dr. Dispenza speak, I felt this overwhelming connection, as if the Universe had brought me to that seminar for a reason, to remind me that I had a purpose and wasn't meant to give up, just like my father and Dr. Dispenza. I realized that none of this was a coincidence. I was exactly where I was meant to be and had more strength than I knew.

After failing that pathology midterm, I decided to try meditation again. Every morning, I woke at 4 a.m. and forced myself to sit in stillness. I started with twenty minutes and worked my way up to an hour, focusing on passing that final exam, visualizing what it would feel like to see the number I needed — 84% — on my Blackboard app. I focused on the excitement, the relief, the sense of accomplishment. I repeated this every day, without fail, even on weekends. And six weeks later, when the final exam results came in, I saw that number staring back at me: 84%. I had passed!

Looking back, I can hardly believe how much power I had given to that specific outcome, but the experience was pivotal. It opened my eyes to how powerfully our thoughts shape our realities. It wasn't just the meditation or the visualization; it was the shift in my belief system, something NET had helped me work through repeatedly. That realization deepened my love for NET even further.

From that point forward, I became obsessed with understanding how my thoughts and emotional blocks prevented me from manifesting everything I wanted. NET showed me that so much of the stress, anxiety, and hopelessness I carried wasn't just about the present moment—it was deeply rooted in emotional traumas and fears from my past. Every time I worked through one of those blocks, I found myself closer to the peaceful person I wanted to be.

Ultimately, it wasn't just the academic knowledge that helped me get through Chiropractic school. It was NET. The supportive community of practitioners and mentors guided me, and I realized that I had the power to overcome the negative thoughts that plagued me. NET didn't just help me manage my anxiety; it allowed me to release it. It gave me the awareness to confront the beliefs stored in my survival, the limbic brain of fear and failure head-on. I faced these emotional traumas that had held me back for so long and discovered my capacity for far greater things than I had ever imagined.

By the time I reached my final year, I was utterly exhausted—emotionally and physically drained as anyone would be in this program. But what surprised me was that I no longer felt the crushing hopelessness and defeat. I was still afraid and anxious about exams, especially the Board Examinations looming ahead, but something had changed. The old weight of despair wasn't suffocating me anymore. The suicidal thoughts had completely disappeared.

And as I stood there, looking at that 84% on my screen, I realized something else: this was just the beginning of a future where I was no longer held back by fear. I could now embrace the challenges ahead with a little more confidence, knowing I had the tools to create the life I wanted. I felt a flutter of gratitude that maybe I was here on Earth for a big reason, and this idea of a purpose was more obtainable than I had ever thought. I have gifts to share, as we all do, and this was a huge realization: I could do anything I set a positive mindset to.

CHAPTER

BUILDING A NEW LIFE

"If someone wishes for good health, one must first ask oneself if he is ready to do away with the reasons for his illness. Only then is it possible to help him."

—Hippocrates

After graduating from Chiropractic school, I imagined stepping into my new career with confidence and purpose, eager to apply everything I had learned. But life, as always, had its plans. Just as I was beginning to build momentum in my practice, the COVID-19 pandemic hit, bringing everything to a standstill. After nine months of progress, our newly established office in Florida ground to a halt, and the steady stream of patients we had been seeing dwindled to a trickle. The sudden pause left me with more time than I knew what to do with, and for the first time in a long while, I found myself searching for ways to stay busy.

That's when I stumbled upon astrology classes. At first, they were nothing more than a distraction—a way to keep my mind occupied during the uncertainty of the pandemic. I signed up for an introductory course with Debra Silverman because I was curious to learn more about myself and perhaps gain some new perspectives. What began as a casual pursuit quickly turned into something much deeper, offering insights that would ultimately shape how I connected with my patients and approached my work.

Through astrology, I discovered things about myself that explained so much of my past struggles. I learned I am naturally not a "brainiac" who thrives on intellectual pursuits but rather an emotional, intuitive person—something I had always sensed but never fully understood or entertained. My instructor wasn't surprised when I told her about my career in chiropractic or my history as a recovering alcoholic. She looked at my natal chart—Pisces Sun, Pisces Moon, and Scorpio Rising—and it all clicked for her.

As we delved deeper into my chart, she asked me, "Did you find school difficult? Was it hard to focus and stay grounded in your studies?" I laughed as she described my entire academic experience to a tee.

For most of my life, I struggled with traditional learning environments. I daydreamed, got lost in my thoughts, and found it hard to focus on concrete tasks like memorizing facts or formulas. In school, I'd often justify the wrong answers on my tests as if I felt bad for them, a trait that baffled my more logic-driven peers. I now realize that part of my struggle with academic settings was more than just about the work—it was about the emotional weight I carried from my educational challenges. But through astrology and healing, I've embraced those moments that shaped who I am today, no matter how painful.

With no Air Element in my chart—none at all—it made sense that intellect, logic, and abstract reasoning didn't come naturally to me. Instead, I was dominated by Water, which governs emotions, intuition, and feelings. This new knowledge was liberating, allowing me to stop comparing myself to others—especially to my husband and colleagues, who seemed to grasp complex material so effortlessly—and embrace my unique strengths. I wasn't unintelligent; I operated on a different wavelength, more attuned to emotions and intuition. This self-awareness brought me peace and transformed how I connected with my patients.

Astrology transcended its personal use and became an integral component of my practice. Understanding my patients' astrological signs and elements provided me with insightful information about their personalities and information processing styles. This knowledge enabled me to tailor my communication to their specific needs, fostering a deeper connection and building trust. In this manner, astrology complemented my work with NET, enriching my understanding of the emotional and psychological aspects of a person's healing journey.

The insights I gained from astrology and how they mirrored what I had learned through NET re-enforced for me that healing goes beyond the physical. It is deeply tied to our emotions, experiences, and, in some cases, the energies we are born with. As I continued to build my practice, this understanding became a cornerstone of my approach, guiding how I treated patients and saw myself.

Graduating from chiropractic school has represented years of hard work, a moment of triumph and relief. And in some ways, it was. I felt a sense of accomplishment knowing I had overcome my doubts, worked through my struggles, and emerged stronger on the other side. However, as I transitioned from student to professional, I quickly realized that my real learning had only begun. Stepping into the world as a doctor was both exciting and daunting. There was the thrill of finally being able to help others in the way I had always dreamed, but also the weight of responsibility that came with it. Lives would be in my hands now, and I had to be ready.

I was very excited to get into practice and start helping people! Yet, I was equally terrified. I remember walking into my practice for the first time, realizing I was now on my own—with no professor or staff doctor in the room to guide my decisions. I had to figure it out, and that realization hit me hard.

Suddenly, I didn't feel as strong in my ability to adjust my patients. I was filled with a terrifying fear of making a mistake, of potentially hurting someone. Doubts crept in: Had I retained the right information? Could I accurately diagnose and guide someone to health?

To make matters worse, I wasn't just working alone. I was practicing alongside two of my mentors—doctors I admired and viewed as brilliant—and my husband—one of the most brilliant doctors I've ever known. It felt like I had stepped into an entirely new dimension of stress and self-doubt. Why would anyone want to see me when they could see these three incredible doctors? I recall my self-talk darkening and doubtful voices growing louder, questioning my place here. Amidst this, the pandemic struck, with patients canceling appointments. Though I knew it was beyond my control, it felt like a personal defeat.

Despite these challenges, some amazing patient experiences kept me grounded, pulling me out of my insecurities and reminding me why this path has chosen me. One of my earliest patients was a woman with debilitating night terrors. Her episodes were so intense that she would wake up paralyzed for up to forty-five minutes, unable to move. She had tried everything, including holistic treatments and medicine, but nothing worked.

I was intimidated and unsure if I could help her when others had failed. But, after just six weeks of NET, she came in one day looking completely different. She shared that the previous night, she had woken up after a night terror. Instead of being stuck in paralysis, she found herself standing in her kitchen, using the NET homeopathy remedies I had recommended. She wasn't paralyzed! I couldn't believe it! It was such a powerful confirmation that this work had the potential to change lives in ways I hadn't fully realized.

Another unforgettable case was a man with tremors. He had been getting treatment from my husband and was experiencing some amazing improvements in his health journey. After his first (and admittedly skeptical) NET session with me, he came back raving about how much less irritated he felt with his wife. It wasn't just the tremors—his whole emotional state was shifting! I looked forward to each one, eager to hear what subtle but significant changes he had experienced in his life. It was these wins—these moments of transformation—that began to remind me why I was here, despite my fears.

Not every patient had such profound shifts; I had to accept that. "Detach from the outcome," I heard often from my mentors. Some cases were victories, like the man with tremors or the woman with night terrors, but others were more gradual, more difficult. I learned that not everyone is ready for or congruent with healing. People often come in identifying with their diagnoses, sometimes with multiple diagnoses, and while most want to heal, a few are so attached to the identity that their illness gives them that they don't respond as quickly. A woman I worked with was having bladder issues, and though all her scans, labs, and testing showed she was fine, her doctor told her it was all in her head, and there was nothing physically wrong with her. But she was convinced there was something wrong with her. After our examination, I concurred, and we started NET sessions and adjustments.

After two months, not much had changed for her, and she stopped treatment. I was very frustrated that I couldn't help her release the emotional stress her body was holding on to. She was one of the more difficult patients to work with, as every time I would take her through the process, she would say she had already done therapy for some of the memories that came up in our sessions. She refused to connect and resisted that her past trauma and stress could have anything to do with her bladder not functioning properly. She came back to me after a couple of years and had some profound changes with care within a few weeks. She was finally at a place to release the resistance to her own healing. Not everyone is ready to release from the identity they form with their diagnosis. And that is okay! Healing isn't just about the body. It's about the mind—often the biggest obstacle.

As time went on, things began to stabilize. I noticed a shift about a year and a half after the pandemic hit. My practice was starting to pick up slowly but surely. I had wanted to build a referral-based practice from the beginning—I never enjoyed the marketing and sales aspects. I wanted patients to be drawn to me because they needed the care I offered, not because of some flashy advertisement. And sure enough, as I focused my energy on the patients I had, the referrals began to come in.

Mostly, I started seeing women between 20 and 60 searching for themselves, looking to heal from the emotional and physical burdens holding them back. These women, in many ways, reflected me. I knew their struggles and pain, and it was exciting to see them transform as they allowed their innate intelligence to guide their healing journey.

Of course, not all cases were successful. Some patients couldn't achieve their goals, and I had to accept that not everyone is ready for deep, emotional healing. Sometimes, the biggest hurdle is letting go of the idea that they're "broken." I knew a thing or two about that.

Even though I could see the improvements in their brain health, which controls everything in the body, some patients struggled to envision themselves as anything other than their diagnosis. That, too, taught me a lesson: Healing is a partnership, and the patient has to be ready to step into their potential and give 100% effort to the treatment.

But when it worked—when a patient could break free of those chains—it was magical. It was everything I had hoped this journey would be. Despite all the doubts, the rocky start, and the immense pressure I had placed on myself, I knew I was on the right path. I was meant to be here.

Another patient I remember vividly was a man in his early 40s who had been struggling with debilitating migraines for years. He had tried every conventional treatment, from medications to physical therapy, but nothing provided lasting relief. When he came to us, he was desperate, willing to try anything that might ease the pain. In our first NET session, I noticed that his body was tense, almost as if he were bracing himself for something.

As we worked together, it became clear that he was holding onto deep-seated anger he wasn't even fully aware of. Over time, as we addressed the emotional layers beneath his migraines, the frequency and intensity of his headaches began to decrease. No longer being controlled by these migraines, he is living a life that is more peaceful and less reactive because of the unresolved stress patterns he was able to work through in our sessions.

Cases like these solidified my conviction that healing was an internal process. Although I was aware and believed that healing didn't stem from treating symptoms, we had to delve deep into the root cause of the issue, and frequently, that root lay in emotional or psychological factors. It couldn't be detected on an X-ray or MRI, yet it held just as much validity.

The personal growth I experienced through these early cases was undeniable. Every patient's success felt like a small victory, pushing me to learn and trust my instincts. Witnessing NET's transformative impact on my patients reaffirmed its role in my life. The emotional shifts I saw mirrored my own, showing that my journey was intertwined with theirs. Helping others heal wasn't just about them; it was healing for me, too. Their stories and struggles became my lessons, guiding me to heal alongside them.

There were moments, though, that shattered me. Early on in my journey, I almost quit Chiropractic school altogether. One week, three of my colleagues disclosed in their sessions with me that a family member, a close family friend, or a coach had molested them. Hearing that and knowing how widespread such trauma was utterly broke me. I sobbed for days, overwhelmed by the weight of their pain and the realization that this kind of suffering was more common than I had ever imagined. I was more sheltered than I realized growing up. I began to wonder—was I strong enough to carry this? Could I bear witness to this darkness without being consumed by it?

Yet, slowly, the answers came. Those same people, the ones who had shared their deepest scars, returned to me lighter. They told me they felt more empowered and less burdened by the trauma that had haunted them for years or even decades. It was in those moments that my purpose solidified. I understood that this work—helping people release the stress locked in their nervous systems—was desperately needed. I no longer assumed people hadn't experienced abuse; instead, I assumed they had, until proven otherwise. The work became not just important—it became essential.

Balancing the emotional demands of this work was a challenge of its own. The stories I heard were often gut-wrenching, and, as an empath, I found myself wanting to absorb their pain, to take it from them so they wouldn't have to carry it anymore. But I quickly learned that wasn't sustainable. I saw my husband, who works with brain injury patients, fall ill because he was not protecting his energy and taking on too much of others' pain. We realized then that empathy, while a beautiful gift, requires boundaries. One of our mentors, Dr. Len Wisneski, taught us an invaluable lesson: help people out of the pit, but do not jump into it with them. Every person has their journey and lessons to learn. If I were to take their pain, I would be robbing them of the growth they were meant to experience.

I took this lesson seriously and, as my practice grew, I reflected on the joy of helping others find their way. There's something gratifying about being a part of someone's healing journey, knowing that you played a role in assisting them to overcome their struggles. The fulfillment I felt wasn't just professional but personal, too. It was as if every patient's progress reflected my growth, each success story reinforcing that I was living out my purpose.

I've finally found my purpose. From struggling with depression and anxiety to becoming a chiropractor, I've integrated my experiences and training into something meaningful. Sharing my story of alcoholism and isolation in public talks has empowered me. Connecting with others who felt alone, as I did, has been life-changing. My pain and journey weren't just personal; they prepared me to help others on their paths.

In those moments, I often thought back to the advice from mentors during my time in school, the lessons I had learned from NET, and the insights I gained through astrology. All of it had shaped me into the person I was becoming, not just a chiropractor but a healer in the truest sense. As I moved forward, building a new life for myself and helping guide my patients, I realized that the greatest gift I could offer was not just my knowledge or my skills but my ability to connect—to understand the depths of another person's pain and maybe help guide them toward healing with that experience.

This is my journey now: living in my purpose, sharing my story, and helping others release the burdens that keep them from fully living. It is the hardest and most rewarding work I could imagine doing.

CHAPTER

SHARING THE JOURNEY

"Sometimes, the most powerful way to heal is to share the parts of yourself you thought you had to keep hidden."

—Unknown

Sharing my journey hasn't been easy. Talking about my struggles, my pain, and my growth is one of the most vulnerable things I've ever done. There's something terrifying about opening up to an audience and revealing parts of myself that were once deeply hidden. Even now, the thought of standing on stage or writing words to share my story evokes all those fears: the fear of being judged, misunderstood, or rejected. However, I've come to realize that the most challenging stories to tell are often the ones that require the most attention and understanding.

I remember exactly when I took the first step toward sharing my journey. During my 12th quarter of chiropractic school, I was told about a competition coming up called "Talk the Tic," a chiropractic competition to speak about your reason for getting into this field and share why chiropractic is important to you. At that point, public speaking was merely an idea I dabbled in, but I had never truly committed to it. I certainly enjoyed motivating others and envisioning myself as a voice of inspiration. However, those were merely fleeting thoughts that were swiftly dismissed by self-doubt.

"Who am I to inspire anyone?" I would think.

I was so busy with school, board exams, and daily life that I would push those dreams aside and bury them under my hectic schedule. However, my husband encouraged me to sign up for the competition. He saw something in me that I didn't yet. He knew I had a story to tell and that maybe, just maybe, I could help others with it. At first, I brushed off the suggestion, but his encouragement was persistent. He knew how much I admired motivational speakers and loved talking and sharing stories. He believed in my potential to become someone who spoke to and inspired others.

I had watched my husband transform through his journey of public speaking. When he first got up on stage, he was so nervous, pacing back and forth as he spoke about his paralysis injury from when he was just 16. His voice would tremble, and sometimes, he would choke up, struggling to get through telling his story without breaking down.

But over the years, I saw his growth. He became more confident and more grounded. He didn't shy away from his emotions but learned to channel them, turning a tragic experience into a powerful message of resilience and strength. Witnessing his transformation was inspiring and gave me hope that I, too, could find the courage to speak my truth.

So, with all this encouragement swirling around me, I decided to give it a shot. I signed up for Talk the Tic and sat down to write my speech. But as soon as I began, I realized how difficult it would be.

What would I talk about? My reason for chiropractic was Neuro Emotional Technique. Should I talk about emotions? My depression? My alcoholism? My suicide attempts?

I kept these stories hidden for so long, shared only with those closest to me. I had opened up to friends about my sobriety to lean on their support, but talking about it openly in front of an audience? That was different. It felt like walking into a room full of strangers and handing them all of my broken pieces, hoping they would understand and not turn away or, worse yet, judge me.

The writing process was brutal. As I put pen to paper, I felt like I was tearing open wounds that had never fully healed. I cried a lot. It's one thing to confront your struggles privately, but it's another to put them into words that others will hear and potentially judge. Each line felt like a battle between wanting to be honest and fearing how my honesty would be received. I worried about how people would react. Would they pity me? Would they think less of me?

Writing my speech was like peeling off years of armor, revealing my true self. It was painful and raw, but freeing. I found joy in transforming my pain into something meaningful, and gratitude in knowing my story might give someone hope. But there was also deep sadness for the lost and struggling person I once was.

When I finally stood in Dr. Gorman's office for my first speaking engagement at Talk the Tic, I felt like my nerves were taking over. I shook like a leaf. It was supposed to be a ten-minute speech, and I clung to my notecards like a lifeline, hoping the words would ground me. But once I started talking about my alcoholism, all the composure I tried to maintain crumbled.

I began crying right there in front of everyone. All the rawness of those memories, the times I had tried to drown my pain, the darkness I had faced—it came rushing back. And pulling myself together was harder than I imagined. I had to pause, breathe, and let those emotions come out.

I opened my talk with, "Hi, my name is Meaghan, and I'm an alcoholic."

It was a straightforward introduction that surprised and amused the audience. They laughed not at me but at my unexpected bluntness. I wasn't hurt; they didn't know what to expect. In fact, their laughter lightened the tension. Later, many apologized, realizing my words were serious.

They were genuinely remorseful, and I reassured them— how could they have known? We never know someone else's story, pain, and struggle. Ever. It was a powerful reminder that we often don't know what others are carrying, and it reminded me to approach everyone with compassion. You never truly know someone's struggles.

After the talk, many people approached me, some with tears in their eyes, to say they had no idea I had faced such darkness. Others, who had struggled silently with alcoholism or suicidal thoughts, asked if they could speak to me privately. It was humbling and incredibly eye-opening. I had put myself in the most vulnerable position possible, talking openly about my struggles, and in turn, reflected others who couldn't speak up. It made me realize how important it is to share openly, as it can change everything for someone who feels utterly alone.

After I graduated, my husband encouraged me to continue speaking. He would teach seminars and four-hour sessions at our yearly CE courses, and I started taking up twenty to thirty minutes of this time to share my story and my passion for emotional health. At first, I felt unsure—would people want to hear this? Would my experiences resonate? They didn't come here to hear my sad story but to learn about neurology! But the feedback I received was beyond anything I could have imagined.

People would approach me at the end of sessions in tears, sharing how my words struck a chord in their lives. Many sought out NET practitioners who could help them break through their emotional barriers, and some reached out to me directly through email, Facebook, or Instagram. It felt surreal, but it was also incredibly validating. There were moments where I would sit back and think, *"Wow. My story mattered to someone."*

We all struggle, and our paths are often full of barriers and signs we don't initially recognize. Sharing my story—whether a small, 10-minute talk or a longer engagement—showed me that sometimes the right message comes at the right time for someone. It's not about perfect timing or a polished speech; it's about realness, being open, and being willing to say, "This is my journey. These are my scars."

Every subsequent engagement left me feeling like I was part of something bigger, a moment of connection that could ripple out and help someone else find their way through. That made every tear, tremble, and moment of vulnerability more than worth it.

The positive feedback I received over time was not just encouraging—it was life-changing. Each comment, tear-filled hug, and heartfelt message I received after sharing my story reinforced something I struggled to believe: my story had value. People would say, "You have no idea how much your words meant to me," or "I never thought anyone else could ever understand what I'm going through." Only I knew because I was that person once, a long time ago.

During one of these moments of connection, the idea of writing a book first came up. A few practitioners I had worked with over the years who had heard me speak would often say, "You need to write a book." I had always dismissed the idea as too big, too daunting.

My husband decided to write his book after it poured out of him unexpectedly one early morning. He woke up at 3 a.m.

on a random workday, sobbing, and began writing. It was like the words had been waiting for twenty years, ready to flow out. The book became his therapy, a way to process his story of tragedy to triumph. His book was about overcoming the odds, being told he would spend his life in a wheelchair, and defying that reality through sheer will and determination.

Whenever I considered writing my own story, it felt insignificant compared to my husband's dramatic physical triumph over seemingly insurmountable odds. My emotional struggles seemed trivial in comparison. He reminded me that many people face depression and anxiety, and we all have stories to share. Sharing my thoughts could help me heal and reach others.

The writing process became a therapeutic form of self-expression. Putting my life into words forced me to gain clarity and a new perspective on my past. As I wrote, I felt myself healing, finding gratitude for my struggles, pride in my victories, and even forgiveness for my failures. I transformed my story from a collection of painful moments into a journey of growth and resilience. This newfound understanding guided me in working with my NET practitioner to heal limiting beliefs and continue my personal growth.

People would reach out, sometimes long after the event, and share how my words had stuck with them and helped them take their first steps toward healing. Many told me they had done years of therapy, as I had, but still felt lost and hopeless, living under their own cloud of despair. Each time people shared their stories, I was shocked at how it ignited memories I needed to reflect on and resolve the triggers still affecting me. Some would thank me for being brave enough to talk about things they couldn't yet bring themselves to say out loud, often bringing me back to moments of my own paralyzed fear, where became the scared little girl who would hide rather than speak up.

And, each time, it felt like a confirmation: writing this book wasn't just something I was doing for myself. It was for those who felt alone in their struggles and thought no one would understand. It was for the person who might pick it up one day and find comfort in knowing they weren't the only one to face the darkness—and could come out stronger on the other side. Looking back, I can see that every piece of feedback and word of encouragement was like a little nudge forward, pushing me to share more, be more vulnerable, and trust that my story could truly make a difference.

It was the push I needed to take my journey from words spoken at little events to words written on a page—so that maybe, just maybe, they could reach even further and help someone out of their pit of darkness.

CHAPTER

Patient Stories

"Every story matters...We are all worthy of telling our stories and having them heard. We all need to be seen and honored in the same way that we all need to breathe."

—Brené Brown

I firmly believe in our innate intelligence—the wisdom of our bodies. Call it intuition, inner guidance, or something else entirely—the label doesn't matter. What's important is that we inherently know things. Our bodies carry the blueprint for life itself, which is not just a biological fact but a spiritual truth.

One of my patients, Kandel, experienced this deeply when working with Neuro Emotional Technique. He shared how a word—"home"—carried a hidden weight he never expected.

As we worked together, his mind first brought up a traumatic memory of a house fire, but as we continued, it became clear that there was something even deeper. He recalled the moment of his birth, born prematurely with underdeveloped lungs, and the sense of being unwanted by those around him. These layers of emotional pain had been carried with him since infancy, creating a tightness in his chest whenever he thought about the word "home." Through NET, Kandel could process those deep emotions, and eventually, the word "home" lost its edge.

Afterward, he wrote to me: "Currently, I can write this recognizing that the word 'home' does not evoke the same visceral response as it did before. I look forward to places that I can continue to call home."

This is just one example of how our bodies hold onto emotional memories, often without conscious awareness. The healing journey is about uncovering these hidden layers, and as Kandel's experience shows, the process can take us to places we never imagined.

No one else can save us. We are responsible for our healing. While practitioners, friends, or mentors can guide us, the real work happens within ourselves, just as it did for Kandel. Every time I sought healing from external sources, I felt more lost and disconnected. It wasn't until I turned inward and confronted my emotional barriers that true healing began.

I'm not saying we don't need help along the way—we absolutely do! But healing begins within us. We are the ones who must confront the barriers, the emotional blocks, and the pain that prevent us from being who we are meant to be.

It's a process of removing those blocks, clearing the obstacles from our path so we can step into the person we are truly designed to be. I don't think it matters what your religious or spiritual beliefs are—most people believe we're placed on Earth with a purpose.

But for most of my young life, I struggled with that idea. I spent years feeling lost, without direction, and many times wishing I hadn't been born at all. Like God had made a mistake in creating me. I often hear something similar from my patients when their worlds seem to crumble around them. The pain and confusion can be intensely overwhelming.

The journey was hard—impossibly hard—but those struggles shaped who I am today. Maybe my difficulties aren't as intense as someone else's, but in my emotional reality, they were huge. And yet, despite all that, here I am—fulfilled, happy, dancing to the beat of my own drum, and in a place where I can help guide others on their journeys.

But let me be clear about something: I don't heal anyone. I don't have the power to do that. What I can do is guide people, offer them tools, and help them navigate their path. They must want it for themselves, just like I had to want it for myself. In my own healing journey, I turned down many different offers of help or guidance. Not because I didn't appreciate it but because I didn't know how to do it at that time. My blocks were deeply emotional, and that's true for most people. I argue this regularly with my husband, who I know sees it in the patients he treats. But not everyone wants to go into the emotional stress that keeps them in their limitations. And that's ok. We must all navigate our waters to find our way out of the storm. As my husband always jokes, "emotions are messy!" Yes, they can be! But confronting them and releasing the power they have to block your growth is worth it.

We carry so much emotional weight—pain, trauma, and unresolved feelings—that it often manifests in our bodies as illness, anxiety, or disease. Each of us faces unique challenges, and there isn't a one-size-fits-all solution to healing. This is why no single doctor or practitioner can "fix" us. The real work is ours to do.

For Carla, the emotional weight she carried for over thirty years manifested as constant fear and hypervigilance. After experiencing a home invasion in the middle of the night, she lived in a state of perpetual anxiety, unable to sleep without checking her house from top to bottom. She tried traditional therapy, but nothing seemed to help. It wasn't until she tried the Neuro Emotional Technique that she felt a profound shift:

"Someone recommended I try NET. Two years later, I am living a normal life."

This is the essence of healing—clearing the emotional blocks that hold us back from living freely. Carla's story is proof that the past, especially unresolved trauma, can keep us stuck until we're ready to confront it. It wasn't about me or the technique of "fixing" her but about helping her release the fear she had been holding on to for decades.

Healing is not a straight line. Often, the emotional roots of our issues are buried deeper than we realize. Mickey experienced this firsthand when she came to my office for a physical issue: trouble lifting with her right arm. A storm of emotions from her childhood surfaced as we worked through NET. She later described it as a life-altering moment:

"I didn't know it then, but this storm would change my life. I started screaming, 'No, no, no!' and the tears poured down. My body remembered something that I had long forgotten. His name was Rick. He lived across the street. I was only a baby and thought he was my friend."

Sometimes, our bodies hold onto memories we are unaware of, but those memories shape our present reality in ways we can't always see. As Mickey's story shows, healing isn't just about physical symptoms—it's about releasing the emotional burdens we didn't even know we were carrying.

Another patient, Dove, faced not only emotional but also physical challenges after battling COVID-19. Fatigue, vertigo, and sensory overload left her bedridden and debilitated. Traditional treatments couldn't reach the emotional components of her condition. But after starting NET, she noticed a shift:

"NET helped quickly pinpoint some unresolved issues that had made me emotionally vulnerable. It was like clearing out the junk in my emotional garage, which allowed me to better cope with what I had been through."

Each person's healing journey is different, but what remains constant is the need to confront the deeper emotional layers that influence our physical and mental states. Our internal work—whether through techniques like NET or other forms of self-reflection and self-help therapies—opens the door to transformation.

We suffer to learn and thrive. After overcoming our suffering, we can help others by guiding them through similar experiences, knowing what it feels like to be in that dark place. Sharing our stories and experiences empowers us to make a difference. Many of my patients now aspire to write books and share their stories. You never know who you can help by being vulnerable and letting your story flow.

If there were one person with all the answers, we'd all be flocking to them, and everyone would be healed! But that's not how life works. There are countless avenues to healing because each of us has a unique path, set of challenges, and gifts to offer the world. Whether you're working in the healing arts, medicine, or any other field—whether you're an artist, an entrepreneur, or someone who creates beauty through landscaping—each of us has a purpose. Our task is to discover what stands in the way of finding that purpose and being able to shine. What are the blocks we need to clear to feel truly fulfilled?

When we can remove those emotional, mental, or physical blocks, we open ourselves up to express the most positive, vibrant version of who we truly are. That's when we start to live fully; from that place, we can help others do the same. So, it's not about being healed by someone else; it's about learning how to tap in and heal ourselves.

People will always be who they are, and it's not our job to change them. When we find ourselves upset by something they do, the real work is in figuring out why we're triggered— why we feel that discomfort in the first place. These reactions are clues, signals pointing to some unresolved stress or emotional wound in our minds and bodies. By understanding our emotional responses, we start to uncover what needs healing within us, and we take ownership of our growth. We can turn our attention inwards, focus on ourselves, and thus live in harmony with others and the world.

That's not to say we need to get along with everyone or form relationships with everyone we encounter. There will naturally be people we feel more drawn to than others, which often comes down to the energy or vibration we're operating at. It's not mystical or abstract—it's simply that their energy aligns with where we're headed or naturally meant to be.

As we heal and raise our vibration, we may find it increasingly difficult to be around people who aren't doing the same inner work. They may feel heavier, stuck, or stagnant. We sense that kind of disconnect more acutely— friendships or romantic partnerships can shift during this process. If one person is committed to personal growth and the other isn't, that divide can widen over time. The person who remains stagnant may pull the other back down if there isn't a conscious effort to bridge that gap or if they aren't open to growing together. It's like trying to move forward while being anchored by someone who refuses to budge.

I've been fortunate to go through this journey with my husband. We aren't always on the same page in our healing processes, but we understand the importance of doing the work individually and together. This awareness has been vital to maintaining our connection even when one of us is evolving faster than the other.

It's about recognizing that growth isn't always a synchronized process, but the willingness to keep moving forward is what matters. Without that mutual commitment, couples often find themselves growing apart. One person's rising energy or vibration can only stay elevated for so long before the weight of the other person's stagnation starts to drag them down.

This dynamic can be compared to how metronomes behave—a phenomenon that has fascinated me for years. If you haven't seen it, I encourage you to look up "32 Metronome Synchronization" on YouTube. When metronomes are placed on a moving surface and started at different times, they gradually sync up despite initially ticking at different speeds. Scientists believe this synchronization happens because of resonant frequencies and energy exchange between them. There's no direct communication between the metronomes, yet they find harmony. To me, it's a perfect analogy for human relationships and interactions.

Similarly, people's energies can sync up on the same wavelength. When two people vibrate at the same frequency, their interactions feel effortless and harmonious. They communicate easily, understand each other intuitively, and seem to bring out the best in one another. On the flip side, there's often friction when two people are on different wavelengths—say, one is highly energetic, and the other is drained or lethargic. Misunderstandings arise, communication breaks down, and both people can feel frustrated or unseen.

Relationships require emotional and energetic balance to function smoothly. It's like trying to tune a radio to a distant station—the signal is weak, static-filled, and eventually, futile. People can only meet you where they are, at their current level of understanding or growth. This doesn't mean they don't care or want the best for you, but rather that they can't connect with your frequency.

Have you ever noticed how, when you're feeling down or stuck in a negative headspace, being around an upbeat and cheerful person can be downright irritating? Their positivity almost feels offensive, and all you want to do is shut them out—or worse, lash out. It's because their higher vibration is clashing with the lower vibration you're in.

But something interesting happens when you begin to heal and raise your frequency. Suddenly, you want to be around those high-energy, positive people. Their vibe becomes infectious in the best possible way. You start to crave their presence because their energy lifts you and reminds you of where you're headed instead of triggering you where you are stuck.

As you progress on your healing journey, you'll likely encounter individuals on similar paths. Your energy acts as a magnet, attracting people operating at a similar frequency. The more you evolve, the more you'll find yourself surrounded by individuals who resonate with the version of yourself you're becoming. Therefore, it's crucial to be mindful of the people you keep close to because your energy and the energies surrounding you significantly influence your healing and growth. They can provide valuable insights into areas where you're stuck and need to break free to facilitate your growth.

Ultimately, life is about recognizing and learning to navigate these energetic dynamics. We can't force others to grow or change; we can only control our path and surround ourselves with those who support our journey. By doing the inner work, clearing emotional blocks, and raising our own vibration, we begin to see the world and our relationships through a new lens that aligns with growth, fulfillment, and harmony.

As we continue on our healing paths, we must remember that we're never truly alone in this journey. Just as metronomes find their rhythm together, so do people, each resonating with their unique frequency. But what's even more profound is the realization that emotional, physical, or spiritual healing is not something abstract or unreachable. It's something that real people experience every day.

To help bring these concepts to life, I want to share some remarkable stories of individuals who have walked their healing journeys. These are real people, my patients, with real challenges who found their way through the pain, fear, and emotional blocks that once held them back. Their stories remind us that while we each have our unique path, we are connected by the universal healing experience.

Patient Stories:

The following stories come from individuals who, like us, faced unique physical and/or emotional challenges. These testimonials illustrate how healing can unfold in unexpected and deeply transformative ways. Each of these patients used Neuro Emotional Technique as part of their journey, but the real transformation came from their willingness to look within, confront their pain, and embrace the process of letting go.

As you read these stories, I hope you find inspiration and a reminder that healing is always possible no matter where you are on your path.

Keren

I discovered NET while I was trying to live with the grief of someone important dying. Even knowing how important the person was to me, I felt like my grief was exaggerated. I tried to distract myself, but everything pushed me back to it — a familiar scent, a glimpse of someone with similar hair, even buying a gallon of milk – some seemed pretty normal, while others were outright ridiculous.

I researched grief for over a year, working to understand better what I was feeling, and stumbled upon NET and the website for the Brain Optimization Institute. Time went on, and there was still no relief from my overwhelming grief. Finally, after over a year of struggling, I called the number and scheduled an appointment.

During my research, I discovered videos of NET patients and even found a clip on an episode of Grey's Anatomy, but I still felt anxious and had no idea what to expect. After a brief intake interview, Dr. Meg performed her first of many NET sessions with me. I felt different when we were done (only a few minutes later). My head and shoulders were no longer trying to carry the world's weight, and I felt free and calm. I felt better than I had possibly in my entire life. I was confused, though – we didn't talk about death or grief. I don't remember exactly what thoughts came to the surface that day, but I remember somehow just knowing that my brain was protecting me from the grief and that the first layer of my emotion onion had been peeled back.

Over the years, I have worked through my grief, childhood abandonment issues, more deaths in the family, work-related stresses, and for a time, how it felt when my first best friend stopped talking to me in the summer before 6th grade - that terrible feeling was buried deep but seemed to be paying quite a bit of rent to live in my head! Layer by layer, I have worked through more problems, issues, and emotions than I could have imagined.

My friends and coworkers continue to comment on the changes they see (all positive feedback), and I have finally learned to handle my big emotions better. I am more in tune with myself and feel like I am finally the designer of my life—exactly how it should be but never was. NET has been monumental in my life, like a secret weapon I wish more people knew about because it truly is life-changing.

Kandel

The word "home" had always carried a subtle, uncomfortable edge for me, something I couldn't quite explain. When I began working with Dr. Meg using Neuro Emotional Technique (NET), I learned that this unease might stem from a deeper issue—something my brain had been trying to protect me from. Initially, as we explored this in our sessions, my mind went to a memory from my teenage years: an electrical fire had destroyed our home, rendering it structurally unsafe. I vividly remembered the charred remains of the place where my family—my mother, stepfather, and three younger siblings—had once lived. Although we were all safely out of the house when the fire occurred, the trauma was intense.

At first, I assumed this memory of the house fire was the source of my discomfort with the word "home." But Dr. Meg sensed that there was something deeper beneath the surface.

As she continued working through NET, I began to experience an unexpected tightness in my chest and a constriction in my breathing. It became clear that "home" wasn't just tied to the fire—it went back even further. We began discussing the circumstances of my birth, which I don't consciously remember but had been told about over the years. I was born prematurely, with underdeveloped lungs, and there was uncertainty about whether I would survive. Adding to this stress, my 15-year-old mother faced pressure from her family to abort me to avoid the challenges of being a low-income teenage mother.

As we continued the session, images from my infancy began to surface in my mind—photos I had seen of myself as a newborn, hooked up to tubes and placed inside an incubator in the NICU. That image of myself, fragile and fighting for survival, had somehow fused with my perception of "home." It was as though my nervous system had carried this memory, this struggle, since birth, influencing how I related to the idea of home. The tightness in my chest made sense—a remnant of my early fight to survive, breathe, and feel safe.

By the end of our session, something had shifted. For the first time, the word "home" no longer triggered my visceral response. I could think of home without the physical discomfort always accompanying it.

I look forward to finding places I can truly call home, physically and emotionally.

There was another time when I sought Dr. Meg's help, feeling overwhelmed and out of control in situations that would normally feel manageable. I had just been promoted to a Director position after my mentor left for a new opportunity. I felt immense pressure to live up to the expectations set by my predecessor, and it began affecting every aspect of my life. My sleep was disturbed, and my mind was consumed with doubt and negative self-talk. It became clear to me that I needed to address the emotional underpinnings of these feelings, and I turned to NET once again.

During our session, we started with general statements and muscle testing, but as we continued, the process became more specific, honing in on the root of my anxiety. Suddenly, a memory came rushing to the surface, hitting me like an emotional wave I hadn't expected. I was fourteen, watching my three-year-old sister while my parents were busy. We were playing a simple game of hide-and-seek—she would "hide," and I would "find" her, often standing right out in the open. She ran into the kitchen at one point, and I heard her scream. I raced in to find her clutching the open metal grates of a hot oven.

I was only ten feet away, but I felt an overwhelming sense of guilt and shame. I had failed to protect someone I loved so dearly. The image of her hands, blistering with bright pink lines, haunted me. I remembered the guilt I carried when she returned from the hospital with her little hands wrapped in bandages, needing skin grafts to heal. The nightmares about that day followed me for years, but I hadn't realized how much I had carried that guilt into my adult life—until this NET session.

The session uncovered that this unresolved guilt had transferred into my professional life, where I felt equally responsible for the well-being of my clinic. I hadn't cried since the day my sister was burned, but that day with Dr. Meg, the emotions poured out of me. For the first time in nearly 15 years, I cried—tears that released a burden I didn't realize I was still carrying.

Since that day, something has changed in me. I began to experience tears of joy for the first time in my conscious memory. I cried at my wedding when my wife and I saw each other before the ceremony. I cried when my sister, now grown, called me to share the news that she had made her high school track team. I cried as I wrote about how relieved I felt to let go of the heavy responsibility I had been carrying for years.

Thanks to NET, I am learning to handle the responsibilities entrusted to me without feeling doomed to failure. I no longer feel the nausea and shame that used to accompany the fear of not being able to protect those I care about. Instead, I feel lighter, more capable, and deeply grateful for the chance to heal.

Carla

Before I met Dr. Meg, I lived in constant fear every day I walked into my house—and every night I tried to sleep. Thirty years ago, an intruder broke into my home at 2 a.m. I'll never forget that night. My cat woke me, walking across my body, just as I saw the bedroom door slowly creak open. I screamed and jumped out of bed, my heart racing. My gun was in the dresser right in front of me. The intruder, who had been crawling into my room, stood up and retreated to the living room, closing the door behind him but staying inside the house. That gave me enough time to grab my gun and go after him.

As I entered the room, he came toward me. I fired. He scrambled out the door, and by the time the police arrived, they found him dead outside.

For 30 years, I tried to live with what happened that night, but I wasn't doing well at all. I couldn't sleep. The paralyzing nightmares were relentless. Whenever I came home after dark, I had to walk through every room in the house, checking closets, looking under beds, and leaving lights on all night. I lived in a constant state of hypervigilance.

I tried traditional talk therapy, but it didn't help to ease my fears. Then, someone recommended I try the Neuro Emotional Technique with Dr. Meg. After we spoke over the phone, she felt confident that NET could help me, and I trusted her warmth and understanding.

Now, two years later, I'm living an everyday life. I sleep through the night. The nightmares are gone. I don't walk through my house in fear anymore.

Rose

Neuro Emotional Technique not only changed my life— it saved it. I was living every day in constant fear of making a mistake. At first, it was small things, like worrying I would offend someone. But that fear grew. Soon, I feared I might unknowingly break the law and get into serious trouble. I spiraled, overanalyzing every past mistake, convinced they would return to haunt me. I was stuck, paralyzed by fear, unable to move forward. My family was suffering, my business was suffering, and I was suffering. I prayed for anything that could help me move past the crippling fear of failure.

When I met Dr. Meg, I had hit rock bottom and was convinced I needed to abandon my career. The path to healing was not quick or easy, but it was the one I needed to take to confront the childhood traumas that were holding me back. I didn't even realize these events had impacted me, some of which I had to strain to recall. But those unresolved feelings were showing up in my present-day life, echoing my fears and anxieties. The child in me cried for help, but I couldn't hear her voice.

NET allowed me to connect with that part of myself, to offer her understanding, and to finally let go. Today, I am thankful I can face adversity without feeling I need to hide or hold my breath. I can look at life's events clearly and develop a path forward. Life is full of ups and downs, but thanks to NET, I have the tools to face challenges with a sound mind and a strong heart.

Serena

When I was 21 years old, I had my first panic attack due to past trauma, which spiraled me into living in a state of 24/7 anxiety. Some of the ways my body reacted to the anxiety were that I was fainting several times a day, had horrible vertigo, my hands and feet would go numb, my heart was constantly racing, and I couldn't take a deep breath.

It got to the point where I couldn't leave my house without feeling like I was going to pass out, so I was stuck in my room for 4 months. I had to quit my job, I couldn't go out with my friends, I couldn't even go to the grocery store. I was scared and depressed. I thought something was physically wrong with my body and I was just going to have to live like this, forever.

I talked to multiple therapists and saw many doctors, and nothing worked for me. I was stuck in a state of fight or flight, and I was miserable.

The first time I went to the office to see Dr. Meg for NET was the first time I had left my house in months. I couldn't even sit in the waiting room; I went into the bathroom, pacing around and splashing my face with cold water, trying not to pass out. I started coming for NET every week. Slowly, the dizziness and anxiety got better with each session. It was scary having to process all of these emotions, but I was willing to do anything it took to get my life back. NET completely saved my life, and I knew I needed to learn it to give to other people what it did for me. To show people that they don't have to live with anxiety and depression.

Today, I am 9 months from starting my internship with Dr. Meg. I went from not even being able to go to the grocery store to being in a doctorate program. None of this would be possible for me without NET. In a weird way, I believe all of this happened to me for a reason. I went through something so scary and horrible, but it brought me NET, and now I get to help people heal.

Dove

I found the Neuro Emotional Technique after spending more than a year primarily bedridden, consumed by severe fear, depression, and anxiety stemming from vertigo and extreme fatigue caused by Long COVID. My condition was so debilitating that I could barely manage basic tasks like hygiene and eating—tasks that someone else had to help with.

Sensory overload was another constant struggle. Even minor sounds, lights, or physical sensations overwhelmed me. Sometimes, simply taking a shower or brushing my teeth was too much. If my husband closed a door too loudly or touched me unexpectedly, my brain would shut down, leaving me crying and writhing in bed for hours until I could calm down.

Before this, I had worked full-time with families of developmentally disabled children. I loved my work—it was both personally and professionally rewarding. Despite the challenges that came with it, including personal health and safety risks, nothing could have prepared me for the anxiety and paralysis that came from being trapped in my body and mind.

It wasn't just fear and anxiety that I was battling—my symptoms were all tangled together, making it hard to separate the physical from the emotional or mental. When my chiropractor recommended that I contact Dr. Michael Longyear for the neurological issues I was facing, it seemed impossible. Their clinic, the Brain Optimization Institute, was a seven-hour drive away, and I could barely leave my house, let alone travel that distance. But I visited their website and read about NET, and for the first time in months, I felt a glimmer of hope. I decided to reach out for a virtual appointment with Dr. Meaghan to see what we could do until I could get to them in person.

At that point, I was slowly starting to regain a little stamina. I had begun seeing an integrative physician whose treatments were helping, though I still had to wear noise-canceling headphones and dark sunglasses to cope with the sensory overload. Even with anti-anxiety medication, going to the doctor's office was exhausting, and I was far from functional. I couldn't drive, and even riding in the car with my eyes open for over a few seconds was too much. When I returned home, all I could do was lie in bed for hours to recover.

During our telehealth sessions, Dr. Meg helped me gradually expand what I could do physically and shift my mindset from constantly preparing for the worst-case scenario to believing I could get my life back. Her unwavering belief in me, her encouragement, and her positive attitude were invaluable—at times, it felt like she was performing CPR on my mental and emotional state.

One of the most transformative exercises Dr. Meg gave me was a creative project: to make a poster depicting the "roadblocks" between me and the road trip to the Brain Optimization Institute. On the poster, I illustrated mountains of anxiety, landslides of sensory overload, and stamina crashes, which were happening almost daily. Each roadblock represented a fear or challenge, and I listed ways to overcome them. It took weeks to complete, as I was still quite limited, but visually representing my fears and how I could surmount them was incredibly empowering.

Only six weeks after starting telehealth sessions, I made the trip to the Brain Optimization Institute for in-person therapy, including neurological treatment with Dr. Michael. That trip was life-changing for me. I finally began to believe in my ability to make real progress. As long as I continued working on the neuro exercises and kept renewing and restoring my mind, I knew I was on the path to healing.

Looking back, I can see how quickly NET helped identify unresolved emotional issues that had left me vulnerable. Each time Dr. Meg pinpointed a past trauma that was still affecting me, I was shocked. It felt like clearing out the mental and emotional clutter that had accumulated over months of isolation and illness. I truly believe that without NET, it would have taken many years of traditional therapy to get to the place where I could function again.

It's now been eight months since those dark days of being stuck in bed with severe fatigue, vertigo, fear, and anxiety. I recently returned from a road trip to visit friends and family. I could hold conversations, visit attractions, handle sensory stimulation, and even drive through a few cities! While my daughter did most of the driving, I could keep my eyes open for much of the trip and enjoy the scenery without triggering vertigo. For the first time in a long time, I wasn't afraid of what the stimulation might do to me, and I felt so proud of myself for facing and overcoming the challenges along the way.

I am profoundly grateful for the support I've received from my family, friends, and the entire team at the Brain Optimization Institute. Most of all, I praise God for guiding me to the care providers who encouraged me to keep going and look for ways to expand my health. This healing journey has been a complete transformation of body, mind, and spirit, and I feel like a new person. I'm excited about what lies ahead in this next chapter of life's adventure!

Mickey

I was introduced to Neuro Emotional Technique somewhat by accident. I had accompanied my husband to Dr. Meg's office for his treatment with her husband, Dr. Mike. While I was there, I casually mentioned that I had a severe neck problem. Dr. Mike asked me to lift a weight with my right arm. I struggled—it felt impossibly heavy. I used to be able to lift 10 pounds without a problem, but now it felt like I could barely move it. Dr. Mike suggested doing NET on my right SCM (sternocleidomastoid muscle). I was skeptical. How could working on a muscle with NET help me lift this weight?

As I sat there with Dr. Meg, she tested me, but I can't tell you the specific statements we went through. What I can tell you is that what followed changed my life. As I sat there with my hand on my forehead, something began to stir inside me—a storm, not outside but within me, brewing in the room, in my mind, and in my body. I didn't know it then, but this storm would alter everything.

The sensation grew louder, more intense. Suddenly, my hands thrust tightly against my head with every bit of force I could muster. I felt the right side of my body heat up, starting from my head and spreading down my neck, shoulder, and chest. My body pulled away from the heat as I leaned to the left, when out of nowhere, I screamed, "No!"

Then it came again—*"No, no, noooo, NOOOOO!"*

Over and over, the words poured out of me. My head shook back and forth as tears streamed down like a floodgate had burst open.

There was a presence next to me, something I could feel but not see, and I needed it gone.

"Get it away," I thought, *"I can't be near it."*

My mind raced with thoughts: What if someone hears me? What is happening? Why can't I stop this? Why won't the tears stop?

My body raged, caught in a wave of fear, pain, and anguish I had never felt before, as if it was protecting itself from something that had haunted me for years.

And then, just as quickly as the storm had begun, it passed. My body cooled and relaxed, and I sat up straight, feeling safe again. The right side of me no longer felt hot or tight—it felt whole. My arms, which had been stiff against my head, relaxed softly at my sides. In a calm voice that surprised me, I looked up at Dr. Meg and said, "His name was Rick. He lived across the street. I was only a baby and thought he was my friend."

After the session, I walked out and lifted that weight with such ease that it startled me.

What just happened? Why was it suddenly so easy? Did they change the weight on me?

As I drove away, I couldn't stop thinking about what had just unfolded. I called my mom and explained everything—

the storm, the cry, and the surfaced memory. I asked her, "Was his name Rick? Did it happen?"

The silence on the other end of the phone was deafening.

Then I heard her voice break as she said, "Oh God. I prayed my whole life, and it didn't happen. I prayed it was just in my head. Honey, I'm so sorry."

I told her, "It's okay, Mom. It really is. I'm okay now."

I had no conscious memory of this life event until that day, but my body had remembered. I don't have a clear picture of what happened, but my body does. Now, I can only see Rick sitting on the front porch, on my right side—the man in the shadows no longer looms over me. His name was Rick, and he didn't get to hold my body in fear anymore. NET and Dr. Meg helped me heal in a way I never knew I needed.

That day, I learned how deeply life events can be stored within the fibers of our being. I learned that something I hadn't consciously known about had been affecting who I was. Most importantly, I learned that I no longer have to carry that fear.

Joan

Neuro Emotional Technique became an unexpected yet essential part of my healing journey. In 2022, I was dealing with a debilitating illness. After countless hospital visits and numerous tests, I was told that this was my "new normal." Doctors advised me to manage my symptoms rather than seek further solutions, but that didn't sit right with me. Determined to find answers, I began researching the connection between the limbic brain and its role in emotional and physical health.

Desperate for relief, I contacted Dr. Meg's office to ask about their experience with my condition. When Dr. Meg called me back, her comforting and knowledgeable demeanor gave me hope for the first time in months. Bedridden and barely able to function, let alone care for my children, I finally felt understood. She was the first healthcare provider I believed could help me regain my health.

During my treatment, Dr. Meg's husband, Dr. Mike, suggested I try NET. Initially, I was skeptical—it seemed a bit "weird" to me. But at that point, I had little to lose. Soon, I discovered just how deeply connected the mind and body are. Emotions I had buried for years were surfacing as physical symptoms—anxiety, panic attacks, exhaustion, and heart palpitations, to name a few.

During my first NET session, as I sat at Dr. Meg's table, she used muscle testing to uncover the root of my issues. I was shocked when she pinpointed the exact age when I had experienced a significant stressful event—something I hadn't thought about in years. As I placed my hand on my forehead and began to process, tears poured down my face. My body felt hot, but it wasn't sadness that overcame me—it was an overwhelming sense of relief. It was as if my body had finally released what I had held onto for so long.

That first session felt like a door had opened in my mind, allowing repressed memories to flood back. I began to process them with newfound clarity. Almost immediately, I noticed a change: triggers that had once sparked anxiety in my daily life no longer elicited the same reaction. I was amazed at the effectiveness of this technique.

Since then, I have had multiple NET treatments, each one offering different results. Some sessions brought immediate relief, while others revealed insights that took time to unfold. During certain visits, I recalled stressful events that I could address, leaving me with a sense of release. In other sessions, even without a clear memory, I began to understand how past experiences had shaped my present anxieties.

NET has become a vital part of my healing journey. Calming my mind has also significantly reduced my physical symptoms and restored my quality of life. Through this process, I've learned that true healing is both mental and physical, and NET has been one of the most transformative tools in helping me reclaim peace in my life.

Cadence

I'll never forget the day I learned about Neuro Emotional Technique (NET). I was sitting in the very back of room CE127, just trying to satisfy my remaining continuing education credits for the year. I had returned to the chiropractic college I had graduated from just 4 years earlier. Now, I usually learn a thing or two at these things, but

I was unaware of how this one talk would change the trajectory of my career… and also my life.

Two of the speakers that evening were Drs. Meaghan and Michael Longyear. Dr. Mike spoke first, giving us all his juicy neurology knowledge. You can tell right off the bat how passionate he is about this topic. The "hard-to-understand" info for the average person to grasp just flows right out of his mouth with such ease. I later found out he's an Aquarius, and in my mind, they are the keepers of knowledge, so that tracks.

When he finished speaking, he gave the floor to Dr. Meg. She started talking about this technique I had never heard of, which was discovered by another chiropractor. So, of course, I'm intrigued. She began sharing a little of her story and her experience with NET. I almost couldn't believe the person I was watching and listening to had the history she did. How could someone so lovely and bright be the same person as the one she was just telling us about? I was fascinated. I mean, "leaned forward, elbows on the table, cheeks resting on my palms, probably stars in my eyes," kind of fascinated.

At the end of their talk, they put up a slide with a documentary titled "Stressed" and encouraged us to watch it to find out more about NET. I went home that night and watched it.

My first thought was, "How did I go through almost 4 years of chiropractic school and not once hear of this technique?" My second thought was, "I have to learn how to do this!".

I was excited about my career path for the first time in a while. I absolutely love what I do, but at that time, my fire was pretty dim. I was going through the motions with no growth in sight. Looking back, this was the glimmer that set so many things in motion. I went on to the NET website to find their seminar schedule and began searching for one close to me.

I signed up for the first seminar I could attend, which was about 5 months later. During that time, I did not seek out a practitioner who did NET to even try it out first. What I had heard was enough for me. So when I showed up to this 3 day seminar to learn this technique, I was also being patient for the first time.

The weekend was like therapy on steroids, and by the end, I didn't know whether to shut down or go around the room and give every person a hug. So much weight that I didn't even know I had been carrying was lifted off my chest, and I felt more clear than I had in years. So many of the unresolved emotions that I had shoved so deep down I didn't even know they were there came back to the surface and were processed again in a safe environment. I decided then and there that I was going to complete the certification that year and become an NET practitioner. And I did. The 2nd seminar I attended was when I finally got to meet the woman who was the catalyst to my NET journey. Dr. Meg. I sought her out in true fangirl fashion and just had to tell her thank you! Since then, she's become one of my favorite people on the planet, and I'm so incredibly thankful to call her my mentor and friend.

Kaida

As a chiropractor, I understood how emotions could cause "subluxations" according to the three Ts principles. However, from a young age, I was taught to suppress my emotions, viewing them as a weakness. This emotional repression led to conditions like hand shaking, anxiety, IBS, and headaches. I also experienced sensory issues and post-concussive challenges, for which I would travel to see Dr. Michael Longyear a few times a year for functional neurological care. I remember Dr. Meg telling me how she would love to do some NET with me sometime. I would kindly laugh and explain that I didn't want to go anywhere near my emotions.

I visited Drs. Longyear again, more open to new approaches. Dr. Meg muscle tested me for emotions using frequency vials, and "rejection" surfaced as the most significant trigger. She gave me a small crystal rock programmed with "self-love" and suggested I try NET. Surprisingly, I agreed. Within minutes, she found an event tied to rejection when I was 18, and as memories surfaced, I felt a shift. The crystal rock, representing self-love, had likely opened me to this healing process.

After this session, I noticed immediate changes. Scenarios that would have triggered rejection or caused me to shut down felt different. Over the years, NET has helped me address emotional roots that were often the missing link in my physical health. Eye movements, joint issues, and other conditions improved alongside my emotional healing.

More importantly, I became a different person—not just physically but emotionally and relationally. The emotional triggers that once distorted my perceptions and reactions were no longer in control. NET allowed me to step back, observe clearly, and respond with intention rather than reactivity. It didn't just heal my body—it reshaped my entire life. Emotions were not just abstract nuisances; they were the key to my healing and transformation.

CHAPTER

MOVING FORWARD WITH HOPE

"If you can't fly, then run. If you can't run, then walk. If you can't walk, then crawl, but whatever you do, you have to keep moving forward."

-Martin Luther King, Jr.

When I look back at the lessons I've gained from my personal and professional journey, a few key themes stand out: the power of resilience, the importance of vulnerability, and the profound capacity of the human heart to heal. These lessons have transformed how I approach my life and engage with those around me, especially my patients.

Life, with its many challenges, can often feel overwhelming. Sometimes, I felt like giving up, and in the darkest moments, I questioned my ability to keep living. But as I reflect, I understand that resilience allowed me to push through each time I felt I had reached my limit.

Resilience doesn't mean that we don't stumble or feel pain; instead, it's the ability to rise after every fall, no matter how hard the landing. Learning to be resilient has shown me that I am capable of far more than I ever believed.

For so long, I thought I needed to be strong, hide my struggles, and present an image of perfection. But I've learned that true strength comes from being open about our challenges and letting others see us in our raw, authentic form. Vulnerability, though initially terrifying, has become one of the most liberating aspects of my life. It allows me to connect with others on a deeper level, not only as a professional but as a human being. Sharing my story, my struggles with mental health, and my battles has been one of the most empowering decisions I've made, both for myself and for those who have found solace in my words.

Working as a chiropractor has been deeply fulfilling in my professional life, but I've discovered that my role extends beyond physical healing. My experiences have shown me that health also has emotional and psychological dimensions. Pain, whether physical or emotional, often has multiple layers, and true healing isn't just about addressing what's physically broken; it's about supporting the whole person.

This holistic approach has transformed my practice, enabling me to understand my patients' emotional struggles—many of which I can relate to on a personal level—and allowing me to support them not only as a doctor but also as a fellow traveler on the path to healing.

This understanding brought me back to the core philosophy of chiropractic, as laid out by D.D. Palmer, the founder of the field. He identified the three underlying causes of subluxation, or nerve interference, as the 3 T's: thoughts, trauma, and toxins. While my education thoroughly covered the physical aspects of trauma and toxins, I always wondered why the role of "thoughts" was mainly left unaddressed. It struck me as a significant gap, especially given that a chiropractor created the Neuro Emotional Technique decades ago—a method that directly addresses the impact of emotional stress on the body.

My passion for integrating this mind-body connection into our curriculum has grown, driving my mission to establish an NET elective on chiropractic campuses. I firmly believe that equipping future chiropractors with this knowledge can broaden our impact and truly enhance the lives of the people we serve. Too many practitioners have shared with me that they had never heard of NET, and I'm determined to change that.

My journey of personal growth is far from over, and every day brings new opportunities to learn, evolve, and refine my skills. The lessons I've gained in resilience, empathy, and vulnerability have laid a strong foundation for continuous self-improvement. I remain committed to becoming the best version of myself as a healthcare professional and an individual dedicated to making a difference in the world.

Moving forward, we want to expand our practice, not just in terms of the services our office offers but also in terms of the scope of our impact on the community. We envision creating a space where people can come for physical healing and emotional and mental support. We hope to build a comprehensive wellness center that integrates more holistic approaches to address the multifaceted nature of health.

In the years since I first tried to speak publicly, I have had the privilege of talking to groups about my story and knowledge of mind-body stress, and the response has been amazing! People have told me how my words have resonated with them and how they've felt less alone in their struggles. This has been one of the most rewarding experiences of my life, and it has ignited a passion for sharing my story on a larger platform.

I plan to dedicate more time to public speaking in the future, intending to reach a wider audience. There is such power in storytelling, in sharing our raw, unfiltered parts with others. It fosters connection and understanding and lets people know that no matter how dark the path may seem, there is always light at the end. I want to spread that message of hope, resilience, and healing to as many people as possible, especially those who feel alone like I did.

There is a deep need for conversations around mental health, resilience, and the interconnectedness of physical and emotional well-being. I want to be a part of that dialogue. By continuing to share my story, I hope to inspire others to embrace their vulnerabilities and find the strength within themselves to move forward with hope.

I plan to continue learning and developing new skills to enhance my ability to serve others. This includes further education in holistic health practices, mental health awareness, and other complementary therapies that can be integrated into my chiropractic care. My goal is to create a space where people feel supported in every aspect of their health journey, from the physical to the emotional to the spiritual.

As I think about the future, I am reminded of the importance of balance. While I am driven to achieve these professional goals, I also understand the need to nurture my well-being. Self-care is vital to personal growth, and I am committed to maintaining a healthy balance between my work and personal life. After all, I cannot effectively help others without caring for myself. I teach this to my patients, and would be a fraud if I didn't apply it to myself, as well! Thankfully, I have doctors I see who remind me when I get too caught up in work, like most of us can easily do from time to time. This is a lesson I have learned the hard way over the years, but it is one that I carry with me as I move forward. I hope to inspire others to do the same.

In moments of reflection, I often return to the idea of hope. When we have hope, we can endure and keep pushing forward even when the road seems impossible. Hope allows us to see beyond the present moment and envision a future where things are better, brighter, and full of possibilities.

As I close this chapter and look toward the future, I want to leave you with a message of hope and resilience. No matter where you are in your journey or how difficult things may seem, know that you are *not* alone. There is always a way forward, a possibility for growth and healing, and *hope*. The path may be difficult, but it is worth walking—or crawling! And as you move forward, carry with you the belief that you can overcome whatever challenges lie ahead.

In the words of Desmond Tutu, "Hope is being able to see that there is light despite all of the darkness."

This quote resonates deeply because it encapsulates what I have learned on my journey. For so long, I felt like I was living under a dark gray cloud that wouldn't shift. Now, the immense light I see and feel is exhilarating. The baggage I worked through and released from my mind, body, and spirit. Life will inevitably bring challenges, but within each of us lies the strength to overcome. There is always hope, even in the darkest of times, and with hope comes the endless possibility of a better tomorrow. Even when you cannot see it yet, it's there. Just keep moving forward!

Abraham Hicks said: "If we were talking to you on your first day here, we would say, 'Welcome to planet Earth. There is nothing you cannot be, do, or have, and your work here, your lifetime career, is to seek joy. The purpose of your life is joy."

As I continue to move forward, my heart is full of gratitude for the lessons I have learned, the people who I have encountered, and the opportunities that lie ahead. I am excited to continue growing personally and professionally and use my experiences to help others. This journey is far from over, and I am full of joy and ready to face whatever comes next with hope, resilience, and an unwavering commitment to healing and growth.

Made in the USA
Columbia, SC
20 June 2025